# Robot Operating System (ROS) for Absolute Beginners

## Robotics Programming Made Easy

Lentin Joseph

Apress®

*Robot Operating System (ROS) for Absolute Beginners: Robotics Programming Made Easy*

Lentin Joseph
Cheerakathil House
Aluva, Kerala, India

ISBN-13 (pbk): 978-1-4842-3404-4      ISBN-13 (electronic): 978-1-4842-3405-1
https://doi.org/10.1007/978-1-4842-3405-1

Library of Congress Control Number: 2018945056

Managing Director, Apress Media LLC: Welmoed Spahr
Acquisitions Editor: Natalie Pao
Development Editor: James Markham
Coordinating Editor: Jessica Vakili

Cover designed by eStudioCalamar

Cover image designed by Freepik (www.freepik.com)

Distributed to the book trade worldwide by Springer Science+Business Media New York, 233 Spring Street, 6th Floor, New York, NY 10013. Phone 1-800-SPRINGER, fax (201) 348-4505, e-mail orders-ny@springer-sbm.com, or visit www.springeronline.com. Apress Media, LLC is a California LLC and the sole member (owner) is Springer Science + Business Media Finance Inc (SSBM Finance Inc). SSBM Finance Inc is a **Delaware** corporation.

For information on translations, please e-mail rights@apress.com, or visit http://www.apress.com/rights-permissions.

Apress titles may be purchased in bulk for academic, corporate, or promotional use. eBook versions and licenses are also available for most titles. For more information, reference our Print and eBook Bulk Sales web page at http://www.apress.com/bulk-sales.

Any source code or other supplementary material referenced by the author in this book is available to readers on GitHub via the book's product page, located at www.apress.com/978-1-4842-3404-4. For more detailed information, please visit http://www.apress.com/source-code.

Printed on acid-free paper

*I dedicate this book to my parents, C. G. Joseph and Jancy Joseph, for giving me strong support in making this project happen.*

The original version of the book FM and Cover was revised. An erratum for the book FM and the Cover can be found at https://doi.org/10.1007/978-1-4842-3405-1_7

# Table of Contents

# About the Author

**Lentin Joseph** is an author and a robotics entrepreneur from India. He runs a robotics software company called Qbotics Labs. He has seven years of experience in the robotics domain, especially in the Robot Operating System, OpenCV, and PCL.

He has authored four books in ROS, including *Learning Robotics Using Python* (Packt Publishing, 2015), *Mastering ROS for Robotics Programming* (first & second edition) (Packt Publishing, 2015), and *ROS Robotics Projects* (Packt Publishing, 2015).

He is currently doing research for the Robotics Institute at Carnegie Mellon University.

# About the Technical Reviewer

**Massimo Nardone** has more than 22 years of experiences in security, web/mobile development, the cloud, and IT architecture. His true IT passions are security and Android.

He has been programming and teaching how to program with Android, Perl, PHP, Java, VB, Python, C/C++, and MySQL for more than 20 years.

He holds a Master of Science degree in computing science from the University of Salerno, Italy.

He has worked as a project manager, software engineer, research engineer, chief security architect, information security manager, PCI/SCADA auditor, and senior lead IT security/cloud/SCADA architect for many years.

His technical skills include security, Android, Cloud, Java, MySQL, Drupal, Cobol, Perl, web and mobile development, MongoDB, D3, Joomla, Couchbase, C/C++, WebGL, Python, Pro Rails, Django CMS, Jekyll, Scratch, and more.

He is currently the chief information security officer (CISO) at Cargotec Oyj.

He worked as a visiting lecturer and supervisor for exercises at the Networking Laboratory of the Helsinki University of Technology (Aalto University). He holds four international patents (in the PKI, SIP, SAML, and Proxy areas).

# CHAPTER 1

# Getting Started with Ubuntu Linux for Robotics

Let's start our journey of programming robots by using the Robot Operating System (ROS). In order to get started with ROS, there are some prerequisites to be satisfied. The prerequisites are to have a good understanding of Linux, especially Ubuntu; a good understanding of Linux shell commands; and Python and C++programming knowledge.

This book discusses all the prerequisite technologies required for robot programming using ROS. This first chapter introduces the Ubuntu operating system, installation, important shell commands, and the important tools for programming robots. If you already work with Ubuntu, you should still go through this chapter. It will refresh your existing understanding of Ubuntu Linux.

## Getting Started with GNU/Linux

Linux is an operating system like Windows 10 or Mac OS. Similar to other operating systems, it has capabilities such as communicating and receiving instructions from users, reading/writing data to the disk drive

© Lentin Joseph 2018
L. Joseph, *Robot Operating System (ROS) for Absolute Beginners*,
https://doi.org/10.1007/978-1-4842-3405-1_1

and executing software applications. The important part of any operating system is the *kernel*. In GNU/Linux system, Linux (`www.linux.org`) is the kernel component. The rest of the components are applications developed by the GNU Project (`www.gnu.org/home.en.html`).

The Linux based OS are inspired from the Unix operating system. The Linux kernel is capable of multitasking in multiuser systems. The good thing is that GNU/Linux is free to use and open source. Users have full control on the operating system, which makes Linux ideal for computer hackers and geeks. Linux is vastly used in servers. The popular Android operating system runs in a Linux kernel. There are many distributions, or flavors, of Linux, which basically uses the Linux kernel as the core component; there are differences in the graphical interface. Some of the most popular Linux distributions are Ubuntu, Debian, and Fedora (see Figure 1-1). The Linux-based operating systems are among the most popular in the world.

***Figure 1-1.*** *Logos of various popular Linux distributions*

## What Is Ubuntu?

Ubuntu (`www.ubuntu.com`) is a popular Linux distribution based on the Debian architecture (`https://en.wikipedia.org/wiki/Debian`). It is freely available for use, and it is open source, so it can be modified according to your application. Ubuntu comes with more than 1,000 pieces of software, including the Linux kernel, a GNOME/KDE desktop environment, and standard desktop applications (word processing, a web browser, spreadsheets, a web server, programming languages, integrated development environment (IDE), and several PC games). Ubuntu can run on desktops and servers. It supports architectures such as Intel x86, AMD-64, ARMv7, and ARMv8 (ARM64). Ubuntu is backed by Canonical Ltd. (`www.canonical.com`), a UK-based company.

## Why Ubuntu for Robotics?

The software is the heart of any robot. A robot application can be run on an operating system that provide functionalities to communicate with robot actuators and sensors. A Linux-based operating system can provide great flexibility to interact with low-level hardware and provide provision to customize the operating system according to the robot application. The advantages of Ubuntu in this context are its responsiveness, lightweight nature, and high degree of security. Beyond these factors, Ubuntu has great community support and there are frequent releases, which makes Ubuntu an updated operating system. Ubuntu also has long-term support (LTS) releases, which provides user support for up to five years. These factors have led the ROS developers to stick to Ubuntu, and it is the only operating that is fully supported by ROS.

The Ubuntu-ROS combination is an ideal choice for programming robots.

## Installing Ubuntu

This section discusses how to install Ubuntu 16.04 LTS. The procedure for installing any Ubuntu version is almost the same. Like any other operating system, a PC should have the recommended system requirements to install Ubuntu. Here are the recommended requirements needed for your PC. After that you can see the detailed procedure of Ubuntu installation.

# Recommended PC Requirements

- 2GHz dual core processor or better

- 2GB system memory

- 25GB of free hard drive space

- a DVD drive or a USB port for the installer media

- Internet access is helpful

# Downloading Ubuntu

The first step is to download the DVD/CD ISO image. To download an Ubuntu image, go to www.ubuntu.com/download/desktop.

You can take a look at all Ubuntu releases at http://releases.ubuntu.com.

The DVD image is less than 1GB. It is named ubuntu-16.04.X-desktop-amd64.iso. By default, the ISO image is 64-bit architecture; if your PC RAM size is less than 4GB, you can use 32-bit architecture.

After downloading the desired Ubuntu image, there are two options for installing Ubuntu.

- Install on a real PC. This can be done using one of two methods. You can burn the image to a DVD or to a USB drive.

- Install in VirtualBox (www.virtualbox.org) or VMWare Workstation (https://my.vmware.com/web/vmware/downloads). With this method, you have to first install VirtualBox software, and then install Ubuntu on top of it. In this book, we prefer this method because it is safe to work with VirtualBox. Installing on a real PC may cause data loss if you don't do it properly. As a beginner, you can experiment with Ubuntu inside VirtualBox.

# Installing VirtualBox

VirtualBox (www.virtualbox.org) is a virtualization software that allows an unmodified operating system (with all of its installed software) to run in a special environment on top of your existing operating system. This environment, called a *virtual machine*, is created by the virtualization software by intercepting access to certain hardware components and certain features. The physical computer is called the *host*, and the virtual machine is called the *guest*. The guest can run on the host computer, which thinks that it's running on a real machine.

You can install VirtualBox on a host PC running Windows, Linux, OS X, or Solaris (www.virtualbox.org/wiki/Downloads). In this chapter, we install it on a Windows PC. You can choose the Windows platform from a list and install it on your Windows PC (see Figure 1-2). The installation of VirtualBox is easy; you may not have any confusing issues. During installation, you are asked to install virtual drivers. You can accept the driver installation.

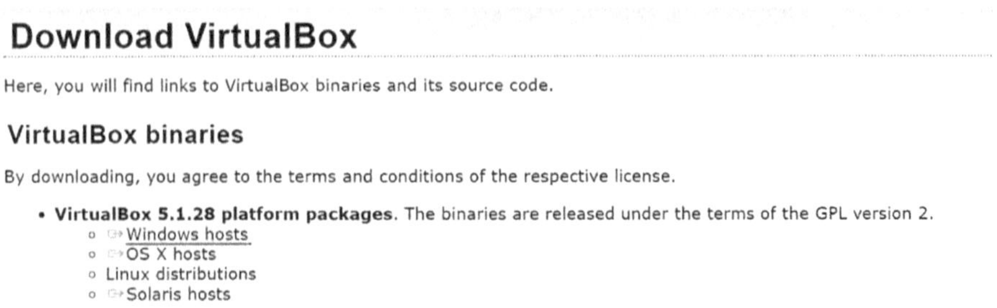

*Figure 1-2.  Downloading the virtual box for Windows host*

If you are working in OS X or Linux, choose the platform accordingly. The installation instructions can be found at www.virtualbox.org/manual/ch02.html.

# Creating a VirtualBox Machine

The first step in installing Ubuntu in VirtualBox is to create a new virtual machine. If you already installed VirtualBox on your system, you can create the virtual machine by going through the following steps.

## Step 1: Adding a New Virtual Machine

After installing VirtualBox on your PC, open it. You see the window shown in Figure 1-3.

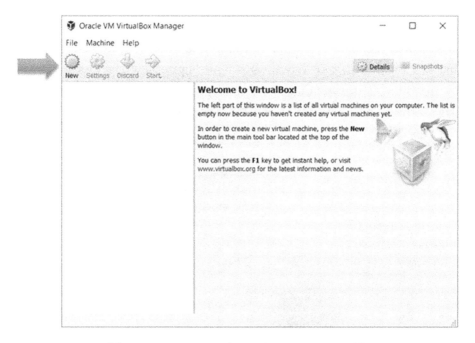

***Figure 1-3.*** *Adding a new virtual machine in virtual box*

You can click the Add button to create a new virtual machine.

## Step 2: Naming the Guest Operating System

After adding the virtual machine, the next step is to name the guest
operating system that we are going to create. As shown in Figure 1-4,
you can name it Ubuntu, set the type as Linux, and the version as 32/64
bit. The naming is just for the information; it is not associated with any
settings. After entering the name, press the Next button to continue to
the next step.

***Figure 1-4.*** *Naming the guest operating system*

## Step 3: Allocating RAM for the Guest OS

In this step, we allocate the RAM for the guest OS (see Figure 1-5). This step is important because if the RAM allocation is too low, the guest OS may take a lot of time to boot, and if the allocation is too high, the RAM for the host OS will also allocate for the guest OS, which may slow down the host OS. So, the RAM allocation should be optimized so that both operating systems get better performance. Based on the RAM size of your host PC, the wizard will show the safety limits of RAM size for the virtual OS in green. The RAM allocation of the guest should be within the safety limits.

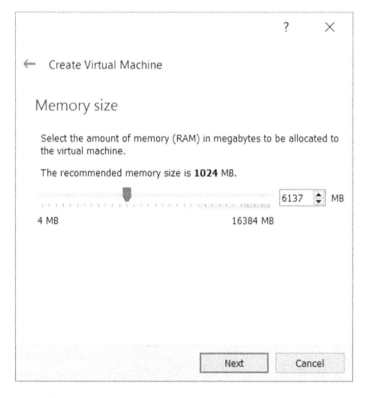

***Figure 1-5.*** *Allocating RAM for the guest OS*

## Step 4: Creating a Virtual Hard Disk

After allocating the RAM, the next step is to create a virtual hard disk for the guest OS. In this step, you can use an existing virtual hard disk file or create a new one. These virtual hard disk files are portable, so you can copy the virtual hard disk to any PC and set up the same virtual machine on that PC.

In this step, you can select the type of virtual hard disk that you want to create (see Figure 1-6). The default option is VDI (VirtualBox disk image), which is the native virtual hard disk of VirtualBox. VHD (virtual hard disk) is developed by VMWare, which is also supported in VirtualBox. The third option is VMDK (virtual machine disk) , which is the Microsoft Virtual PC virtual hard disk type. You can get more information from `www.virtualbox.org/manual/ch05.html`. In this chapter, we are selecting the native hard disk format, or VDI.

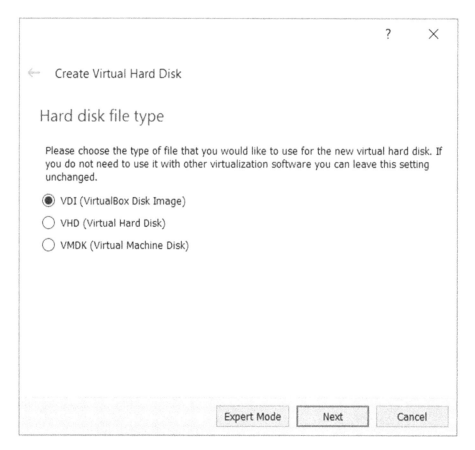

**Figure 1-6.** *Choosing the type of hard disk for the virtual machine*

## Step 5: Configuring the Type of Virtual Disk

In this step, we have to configure the mode of storage. There are two modes: *dynamically allocated* and *fixed size* (see Figure 1-7). If we select fixed size, a virtual hard disk is created with a fixed size. That size can be set in the next step. After creating this virtual hard disk, it will consume that much physical disk size. With a dynamically allocated disk, you can use the maximum hard disk size, and it will only use the physical hard disk space when it fills up. The time taken to create a fixed hard disk is higher than dynamically allocated, but once it is created, it can perform much better than a dynamically allocated mode. In this chapter, we are going to use a fixed size with a maximum size of 20GB.

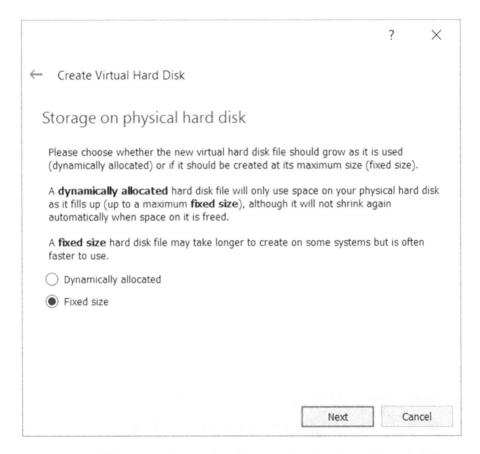

*Figure 1-7.* *Choosing the mode of storage in the virtual hard disk*

You can also browse the location to save the virtual hard disk file. When you finish the virtual disk configuration, it will take some time to build those configurations (see Figure 1-8).

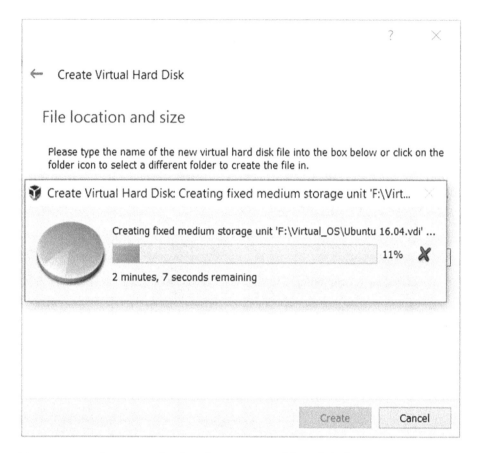

***Figure 1-8.*** *Creating the fixed-size virtual hard disk*

After creating the virtual hard disk, you can see the newly created virtual machine. But where do we put the Ubuntu image in the virtual machine? Well, that is the next step that we are going to do.

## Step 6: Choosing Ubuntu DVD Image

Figure 1-9 shows the newly created virtual machine. We have to select the Settings button to configure the virtual machine.

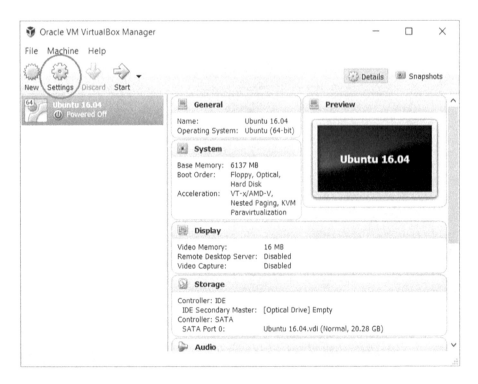

**Figure 1-9.** *Configuring the virtual machine*

In the Settings window, navigate to the Storage option on the left (see Figure 1-10).

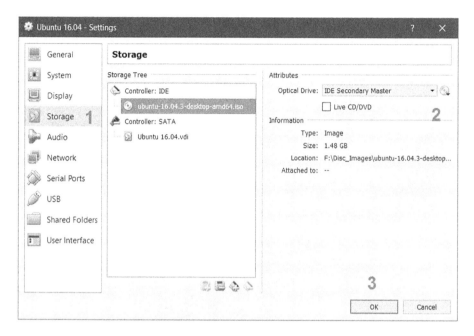

***Figure 1-10.***   *Inserting Ubuntu DVD image in the optical drive*

After inserting the Ubuntu image, configure the video configuration. In this setting, you can allocate the video memory of the guest OS (see Figure 1-11).

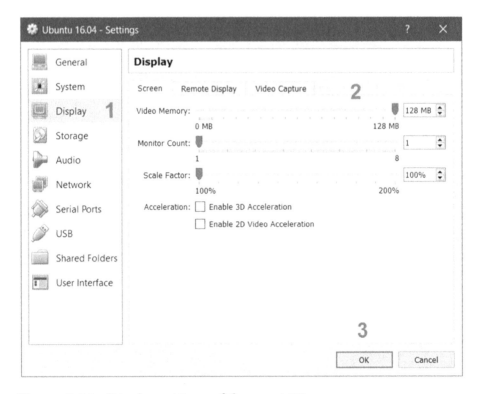

*Figure 1-11.*  *Display settings of the guest OS*

After configuring the Display settings, we have to configure the System settings. In the System settings, you can allocate the number of CPUs for the guest OS. Figure 1-12 shows the safest settings for CPU allocation.

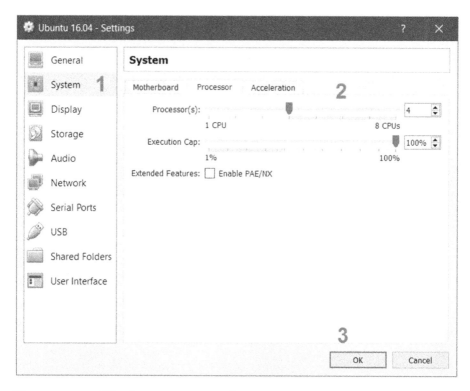

**Figure 1-12.** *The System settings for the guest OS*

The Shared Folders settings may be useful when working with Ubuntu (see Figure 1-13). Using this option, you can share the host operating system folder inside the guest operating system. This option is useful for accessing files and folders from the host operating system.

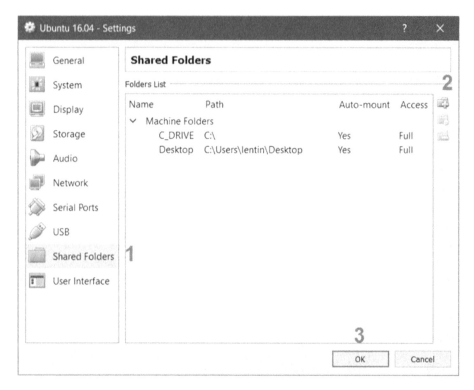

***Figure 1-13.*** *The Shared Folders settings*

After completing these settings, you can start the virtual machine.

## Step 7: Starting Virtual Machine

As shown in Figure 1-14, you can launch the virtual machine by pressing the Start button. This will boot the virtual machine and bring you to the Ubuntu live desktop.

***Figure 1-14.*** *Launching the virtual machine*

On the live desktop, you can explore the Ubuntu features without installing it. You also have the option to install Ubuntu in the live mode. In the next section, we will see how to install Ubuntu in VirtualBox. The steps are the same if you install it on a real PC.

# Installing Ubuntu on VirtualBox

When the virtual machine boots up, you get the window shown in Figure 1-15, which asks you to Try Ubuntu or Install Ubuntu. If you want to use Ubuntu before installing it, select Try Ubuntu, but if you want to directly install Ubuntu, select Install Ubuntu. Here we choose the Install Ubuntu option.

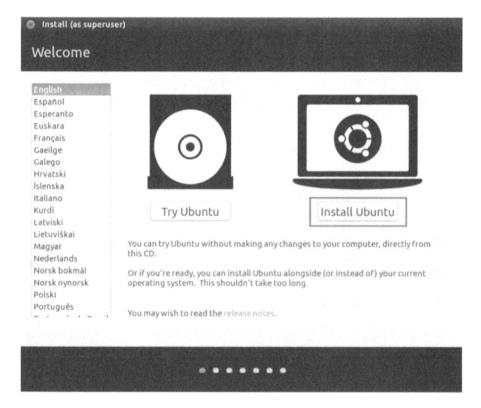

***Figure 1-15.*** *The first window after booting from Ubuntu DVD image*

After selecting the Install Ubuntu option, the next window (see Figure 1-16) allows you to select options such as updating Ubuntu during installation and updating third-party applications and drivers. If you are working in VirtualBox, you can ignore this, but if you are installing on a real PC that has graphics cards like NVDIA or ATi Raedon, you can select these options. It can search for an appropriate graphics driver and install it during the Ubuntu installation; otherwise, you may need to manually install it. However, there is no guarantee that we will get a proper drive for our graphics card.

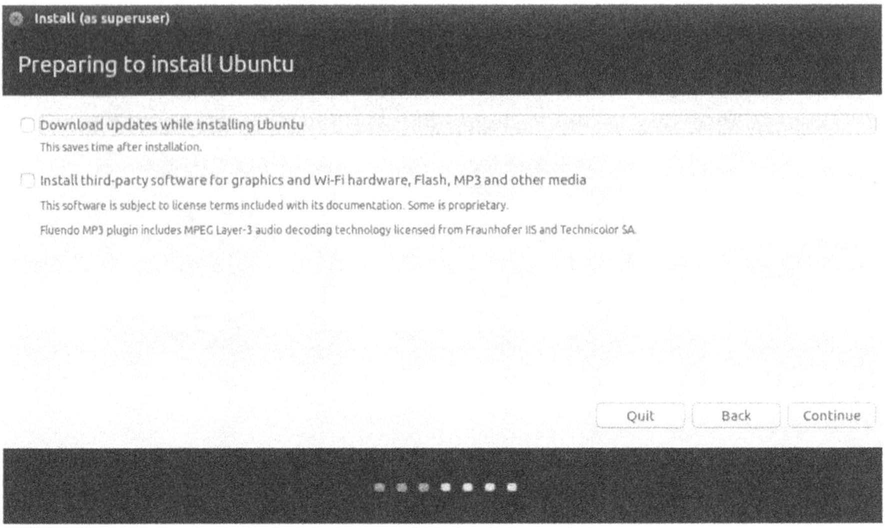

**Figure 1-16.** *Updating Ubuntu and installing third-party software*

After configuring, press Continue to move onto the next step. This step is very important because we are going to partition the hard disk to install Ubuntu on it (see Figure 1-17). You have to be careful when selecting the partition option. The first option, *Erase disk and install Ubuntu*, erases all the drives on the hard disk and installs Ubuntu. If you are willing to do this, you can proceed with that option. If you installed Ubuntu in VirtualBox, this option will be fine, but if you are planning to install Ubuntu along with Windows, select the *Something else* option.

***Figure 1-17.*** *Choosing the installation type*

The *Something else* option gives us the option to format the desired drive and install Ubuntu on it. If you are installing Ubuntu in VirtualBox, you don't need to worry much about this because there is only one hard disk. If you are going to install on your real PC, you have to find a partition for installing Ubuntu before booting into Ubuntu. In the partition manager, you can identify the drive by checking the size of the partition. If the disk is not formatted, you see the disk drive as /dev/sda. The first option is to create a partition table, which you do by clicking the New Partition Table button. After doing this, the disk drive shows free space, as shown in Figure 1-18.

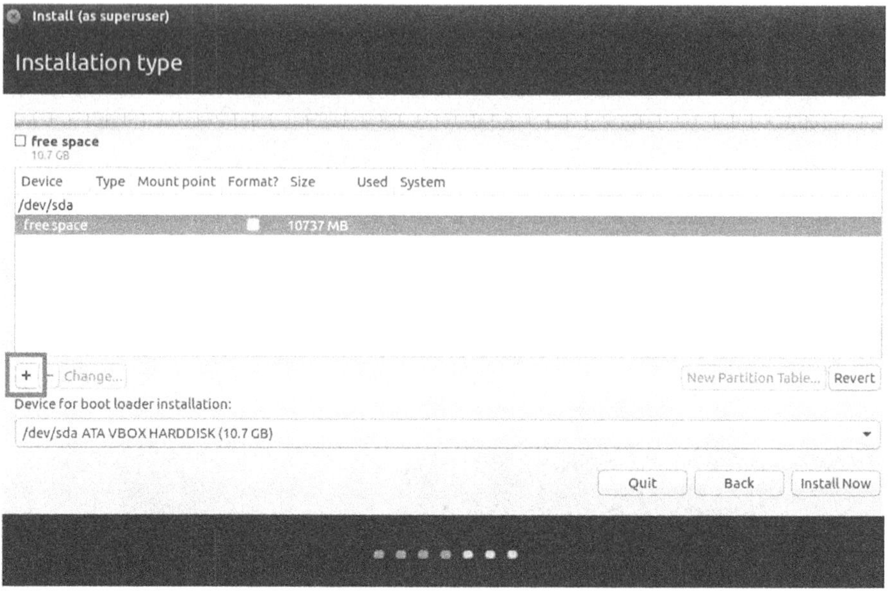

Install (as superuser)

Installation type

☐ free space
10.7 GB

| Device | Type | Mount point | Format? | Size | Used | System |
|--------|------|-------------|---------|------|------|--------|
| /dev/sda | | | | | | |
| free space | | | ■ | 10737 MB | | |

+  −  Change...                                    New Partition Table...  Revert

Device for boot loader installation:

/dev/sda ATA VBOX HARDDISK (10.7 GB)                                    ▼

Quit    Back    Install Now

*Figure 1-18.* *Free space on the hard disk*

You can modify the existing partition with the button on the left. There are three buttons. The button with the + symbol is for creating a new partition from a free space; the button with the – symbol is for deleting an existing partition; and the Change button is for converting an existing partition into another format or changing its size. Here we are going to create a new partition, so click the + button. You see another window (as shown in Figure 1-19), which asks for information about the new partition.

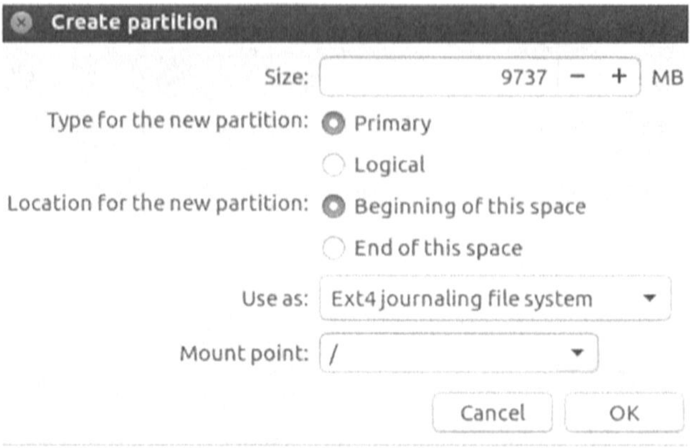

**Figure 1-19.** *Creating a new root partition*

Basically, to install Ubuntu, we need to set up two partitions. One is a root partition and the other is a swap partition. The Ubuntu OS is installed in the root partition. As shown in Figure 1-19, *primary* is the type for the root partition, and the format of the file system is Ext4Journaling. You have to set the mount point of root partition as /.

The swap partition is a special kind of partition that is used for storing inactive pages when your physical memory (RAM) is approaching maximum usage. If your RAM is large enough, let's say greater than 4GB, the swap partition can be ignored; otherwise, it is a good idea to have a swap partition. You can allocate 1GB or 2GB to the swap partition (see Figure 1-20).

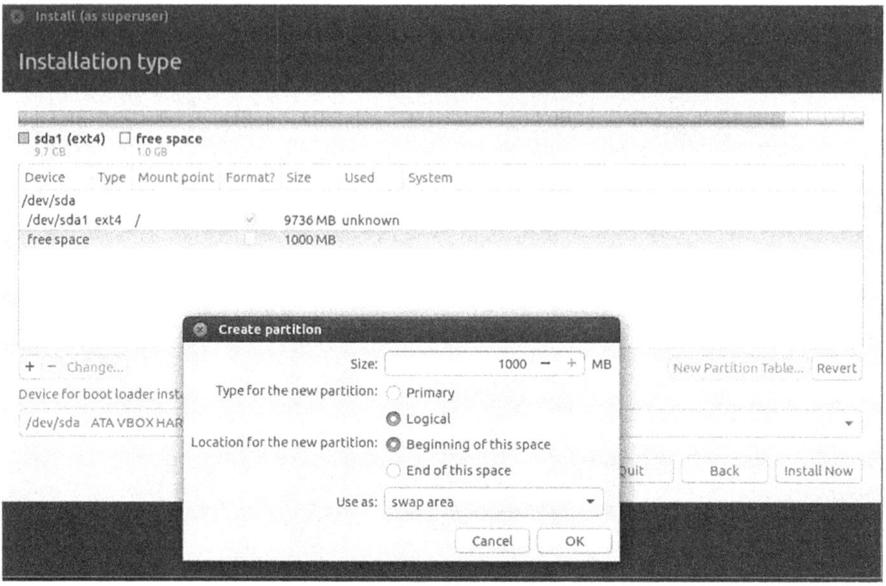

***Figure 1-20.***   *Creating a new swap partition*

After creating both partitions, click the Install Now button, which installs Ubuntu to the selected partition. During installation, you can set the time zone, keyboard layout, and username and password (see Figure 1-21).

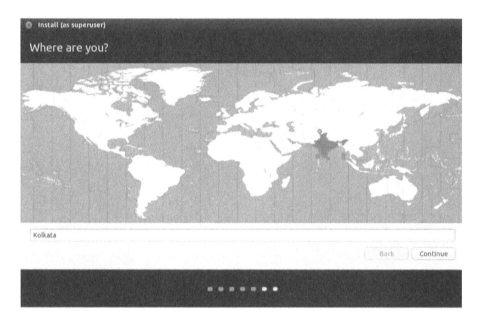

***Figure 1-21.*** *Setting the time zone*

You can click your country to set the time zone. The country name will be visible when you click the map. After setting the time, the next step is to set up the keyboard layout (see Figure 1-22). Use the default keyboard layout (i.e., English (US)).

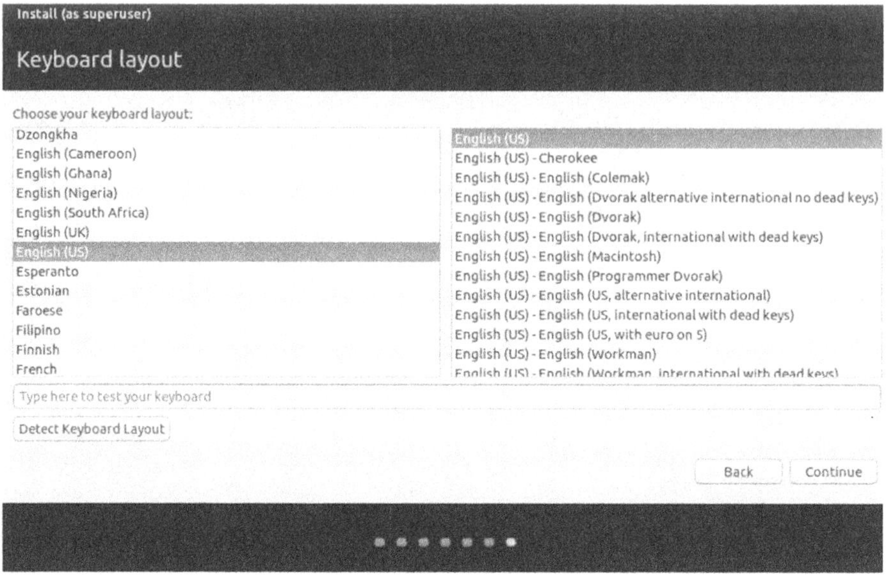

***Figure 1-22.*** *Setting the keyboard layout*

Next, enter the Ubuntu login information (see Figure 1-23).

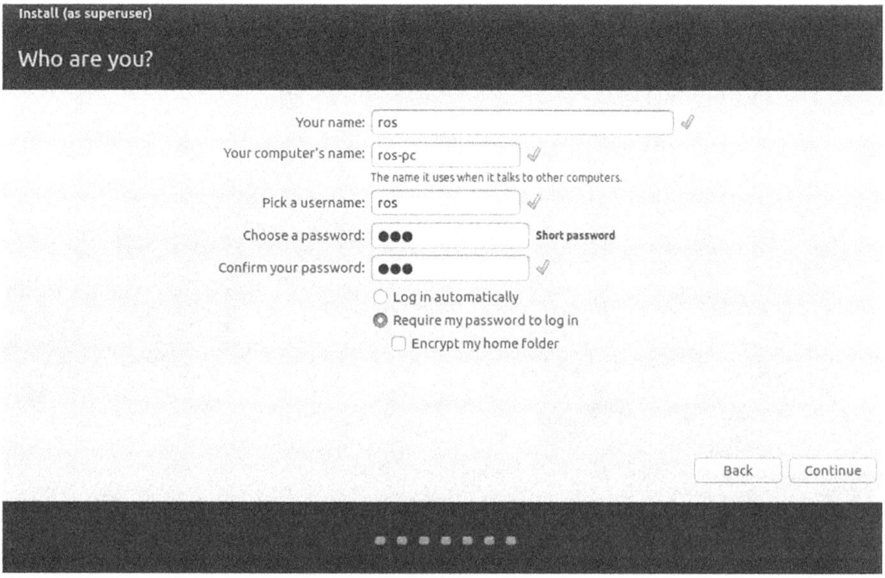

***Figure 1-23.*** *Setting login information*

In this step, we set the PC name, login name, and password. If you don't want to log in using a username and password, you can enable the *Log in automatically* feature. This logs in directly to the Ubuntu screen without prompting for a username and password.

After assigning the login information, the installation procedure is almost over. After installing the files, you need to reboot (see Figure 1-24). Press Reboot to restart the virtual machine/PC. During this time, you can remove the DVD image from the VirtualBox menu. Select Devices ➤ Optical Drives ➤ Remove disk from the VirtualBox drop-down menu.

***Figure 1-24.***  *Restarting Ubuntu*

After rebooting, you see the Ubuntu desktop shown in Figure 1-25.

***Figure 1-25.***  *Ubuntu desktop*

Congratulations. You have successfully installed Ubuntu on VirtualBox. If you are planning to install it on a real PC, you may need to know the following things to boot Ubuntu on a PC.

# Installing Ubuntu on a PC

Basically, there are two ways to boot Ubuntu on a PC. The first method is direct: burn the DVD image you downloaded to a DVD, and then boot it from the DVD. The other method is to boot from a USB drive, which is easier and faster than a DVD installation.

A tool called UNetbootin burns the DVD image to a USB drive. It can be downloaded from https://sourceforge.net/projects/unetbootin/. You can browse the DVD image from this tool. Press OK to start the copying process (see Figure 1-26).

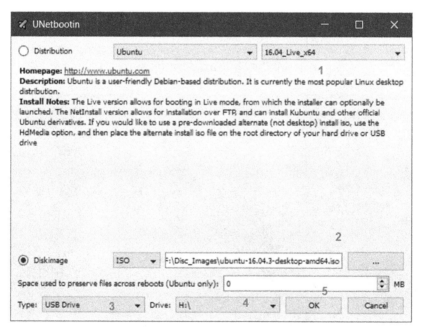

***Figure 1-26.***  *UNetbootin setup*

You can select the Linux distribution and browse the DVD image. After selecting the DVD image, select the type of drive, which is *USB Drive*. Next, select the drive letter. Then, press the OK button. It takes time to copy the DVD image to the drive. When it is complete, reboot the PC and set the first boot device as USB drive. Now it will boot from the USB drive. You can follow the installation procedures described earlier. More instructions are at `https://unetbootin.github.io/`.

If you have any trouble installing the OS using UNetbootin, try Rufus (`https://rufus.akeo.ie/`), which is another application for the same purpose.

# Playing with the Ubuntu Graphical User Interface

On the Ubuntu desktop, there is a panel on the left of the screen called Unity, which is a graphical shell built on the top of GNOME (`www.gnome.org`), the default desktop environment of Ubuntu. It is a free, open source application. The other desktop environments are KDE and LXDE.

Figure 1-27 shows the Unity Launcher, which helps to quickly launch and search Ubuntu applications. Click each app to make it pop up. You can also search by application name. These GUI tools can save your time in finding an application. On the right side of the Unity panel, there are options to adjust the volume and power off the system. The launcher is called the Unity Launcher. The search utility in the launcher is called the Dash. There is an indicator panel to show the network connection, volume, and other notifications.

**Figure 1-27.** *The Unity Launcher panel*

Similar to Windows and OS X, there are many options in Ubuntu for customizing the desktop environment. If you are interested in configuring your Ubuntu desktop, refer to the Compiz Settings Manager at `https://help.ubuntu.com/community/CompositeManager#Compiz`.

To learn more about Ubuntu, download the PDF from `https://ubuntu-manual.org/downloads`.

# The Ubuntu File System

Like the C drive in a Windows operating system, Linux has a special drive for storing system files. It is called the *root file system*, which we created during the installation of Ubuntu. We assigned / for the file system. Figure 1-28 shows the Ubuntu file system architecture.

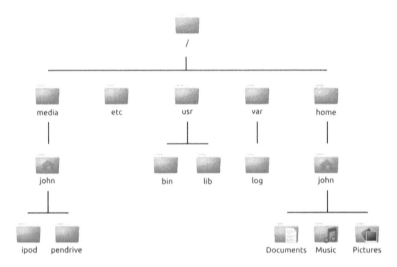

***Figure 1-28.*** *Ubuntu file system structure*

You can explore the file system by choosing File Manager from the Unity Launcher, as shown in Figure 1-29.

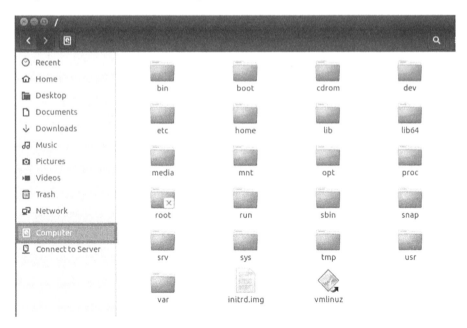

***Figure 1-29.*** *Ubuntu file system structure*

The following describes the uses of each folder in the file system.

- /bin and /sbin: Contains system applications similar to the C:\ Windows folder

- /etc: Contains system configuration files

- /home/*yourysername*: This is equivalent to the C:\Users folder in Windows

- /lib: Contains library files similar to .dll files in Windows

- /media: Removable media is mounted in the directory

- /root: Contains root user files (not the root user file system; root user is the administrator of the Linux system)

- /usr: Pronounced *user*, it contains most of the program files (equivalent to C:\Program Files in Microsoft Windows)

- /var/log: Contains log files written by many applications

- /home/yourusername/Desktop: Contains Ubuntu desktop files

- /mnt: The mounted partitions are shown here

- /boot: Contains the files required to boot

- /dev: Contains Linux device files

- /opt: The location for optionally installed programs (ROS is installed to /opt)

- /sys: Holds the files containing information about the system

# Useful Ubuntu Applications

If you want to install a popular software application in Ubuntu, use Ubuntu Software (see Figure 1-30), which is available in the Unity Launcher. It is a direct way to install applications in Ubuntu. In the coming sections, you see how to install Ubuntu packages using command lines.

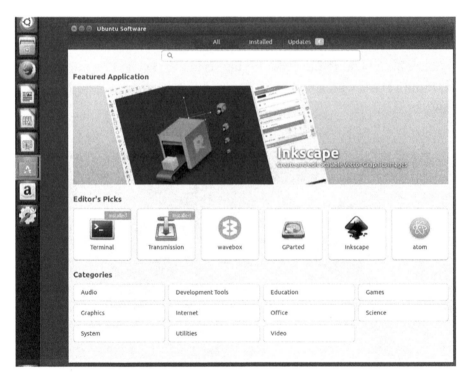

***Figure 1-30.***   *The Ubuntu Software center*

# Getting Started with Shell Commands

The graphical tools in Ubuntu are very easy to use, but if you want to perform advanced tasks in Linux, you may need to learn the Ubuntu command-line interface (CLI). The command-line tools are faster and used often in debugging the system. The command-line interface in Linux can be compared to the disk operating system (DOS) in Windows.

We mainly use the command line when we work with ROS. Knowledge of the Linux terminal commands is a prerequisite for working with ROS.

The Ubuntu command-line interface is in a tool called Terminal. Use the Ubuntu Dash search to find the Terminal application. Figure 1-31 shows an example.

***Figure 1-31.***  *Searching for the Terminal application*

Click Terminal to open the application, which is shown in Figure 1-32.

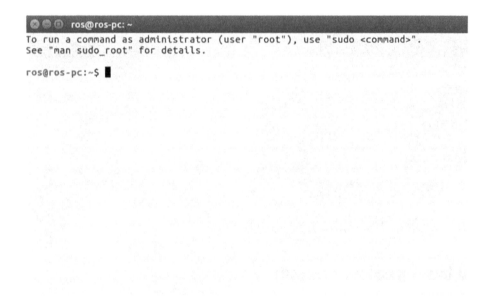

***Figure 1-32.*** *The Ubuntu terminal*

# Terminal Commands Cheat Sheet

This section covers useful shell commands for working with robots and ROS. The following are the popular commands that you want to explore.

## man: Manual Pages for Shell Commands

The man command stands for *manual*. This command provides the manual page of a given command.

---

Usage: man <shell command>

Example: man ls

---

The preceding asks for the manual page of ls. Figure 1-33 shows the output of man ls.

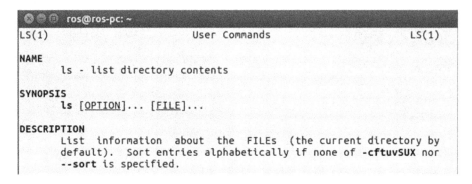

*Figure 1-33.* *The manual page of ls*

# ls: List Directory Content

The ls command lists the content of files and folders in the current directory.

Usage: ls

The output of ls is shown in Figure 1-34.

*Figure 1-34.* *List of files in the current path*

## cd: Change Directory

The cd command switches from one folder to another (see Figure 1-35).

Usage: cd <Directory_path>

Example: cd Desktop

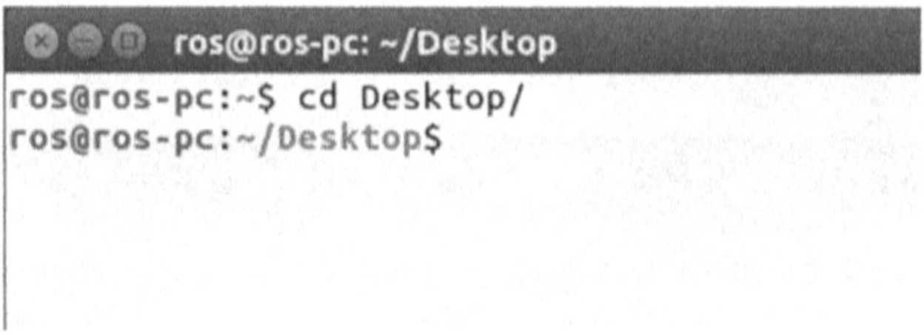

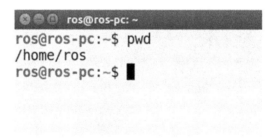

***Figure 1-35.*** *Changing folders*

## pwd: Current Terminal Path

The pwd command returns the current path of the terminal. This is useful for getting the absolute path.

Usage: pwd

Figure 1-36 shows the output of the pwd command.

***Figure 1-36.*** *Command to get current path*

# mkdir: Create a Folder

The mkdir command creates an empty folder or directory.

---

Usage: mkdir <folder_name>

Example: mkdir robot

---

Figure **1-37** shows how to create and list folders.

*Figure 1-37.*  *Creating a new folder*

# rm: Delete a File

The rm command deletes a file.

---

Usage: rm <file_path>

Example: rm test.txt

---

An example is shown Figure 1-38. The files are listed before deletion and after deletion to confirm that the files were actually deleted.

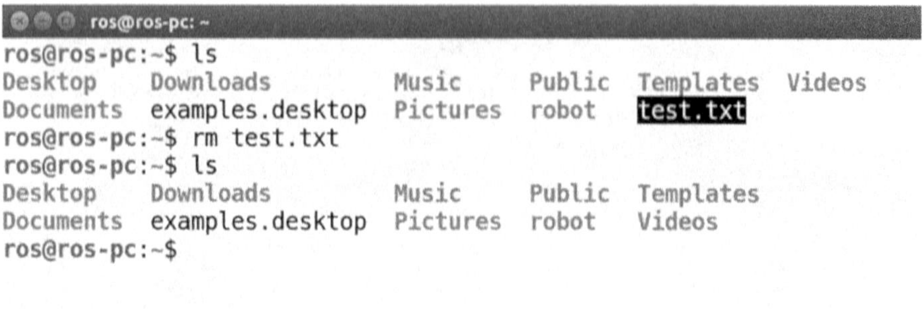

```
◎◎◎  ros@ros-pc: ~
ros@ros-pc:~$ ls
Desktop     Downloads        Music      Public    Templates   Videos
Documents   examples.desktop Pictures   robot     test.txt
ros@ros-pc:~$ rm test.txt
ros@ros-pc:~$ ls
Desktop     Downloads        Music      Public    Templates
Documents   examples.desktop Pictures   robot     Videos
ros@ros-pc:~$
```

***Figure 1-38.***  *Deleting a file*

To delete a folder by recursively deleting its files, use the following command.

```
$ rm -r <folder_name>
```

To delete a file inside the root (/) file system, use sudo before the rm command.

```
$ sudo rm <file_name>
```

## rmdir: Delete a Folder

The rmdir command deletes an empty folder. You may need to delete files before using this command.

---

Usage: rmdir <folder_name>

Example: rmdir robot

---

Figure 1-39 shows an example of this command.

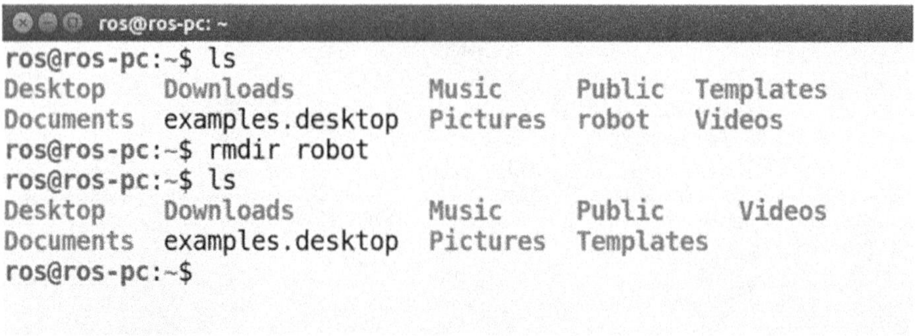

```
●●● ros@ros-pc: ~
ros@ros-pc:~$ ls
Desktop    Downloads        Music    Public    Templates
Documents  examples.desktop Pictures robot     Videos
ros@ros-pc:~$ rmdir robot
ros@ros-pc:~$ ls
Desktop    Downloads        Music    Public        Videos
Documents  examples.desktop Pictures Templates
ros@ros-pc:~$
```

***Figure 1-39.*** *Deleting an empty folder*

# mv: Move a File from One Place to Another

The mv command moves a file from one location to another and then renames the file.

---

Usage: mv source_file destination/destination_file

Example: mv test.txt test_2.txt

---

In Figure **1-40**, test.txt is moved into the same folder under a different name (i.e., test_2.txt).

It is moving the file by renaming the file.

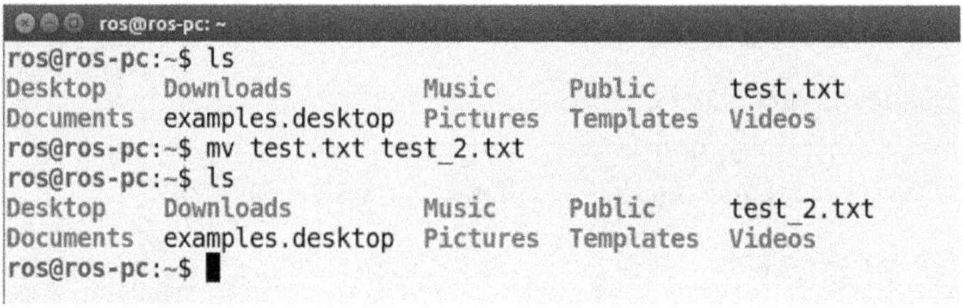

```
●●● ros@ros-pc: ~
ros@ros-pc:~$ ls
Desktop    Downloads        Music    Public    test.txt
Documents  examples.desktop Pictures Templates Videos
ros@ros-pc:~$ mv test.txt test_2.txt
ros@ros-pc:~$ ls
Desktop    Downloads        Music    Public    test_2.txt
Documents  examples.desktop Pictures Templates Videos
ros@ros-pc:~$ ▮
```

***Figure 1-40.*** *Moving a file*

## cp: Copy a File from One Path to Another

The cp command copies files from one location to another.

---

Usage: cp source_file destination_folder/destination_file

Example: cp test.txt test_2.txt

---

Figure 1-41 demonstrates this example.

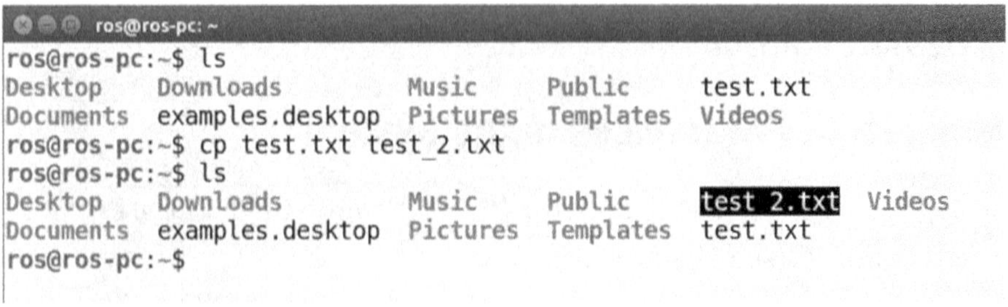

```
⊗ ⊜ ⊜   ros@ros-pc: ~
ros@ros-pc:~$ ls
Desktop    Downloads        Music      Public     test.txt
Documents  examples.desktop Pictures   Templates  Videos
ros@ros-pc:~$ cp test.txt test_2.txt
ros@ros-pc:~$ ls
Desktop    Downloads        Music      Public     test_2.txt  Videos
Documents  examples.desktop Pictures   Templates  test.txt
ros@ros-pc:~$
```

***Figure 1-41.*** *Copying a file*

## dmesg: Display a Kernel Message

The dmesg command is very useful for debugging the system. It displays the kernel logs (see Figure 1-42). From these logs, you can debug the problem.

---

Usage: dmesg

---

```
◉◉◉ ros@ros-pc: ~
ros@ros-pc:~$ dmesg
[    0.000000] Linux version 4.10.0-28-generic (buildd@lgw01-12) (gcc version 5.
4.0 20160609 (Ubuntu 5.4.0-6ubuntu1~16.04.4) ) #32~16.04.2-Ubuntu SMP Thu Jul 20
 10:19:48 UTC 2017 (Ubuntu 4.10.0-28.32~16.04.2-generic 4.10.17)
[    0.000000] Command line: BOOT_IMAGE=/boot/vmlinuz-4.10.0-28-generic root=UUI
D=fa38abcb-2976-4252-ac26-db79f83f21be ro quiet splash
[    0.000000] KERNEL supported cpus:
[    0.000000]   Intel GenuineIntel
[    0.000000]   AMD AuthenticAMD
[    0.000000]   Centaur CentaurHauls
[    0.000000] ------------[ cut here ]------------
[    0.000000] WARNING: CPU: 0 PID: 0 at /build/linux-hwe-vH8Hlo/linux-hwe-4.10.
0/arch/x86/kernel/fpu/xstate.c:595 fpu__init_system_xstate+0x36d/0x99e
[    0.000000] XSAVE consistency problem, dumping leaves
[    0.000000] Modules linked in:
[    0.000000] CPU: 0 PID: 0 Comm: swapper Not tainted 4.10.0-28-generic #32~16.
04.2-Ubuntu
```

*Figure 1-42.* *Checking the kernel logs*

# lspci: List of PCI Devices in the System

The lspci command also debugs the PC. This command lists the PCI
devices in the PC (see Figure 1-43).

---

Usage: lspci

---

```
◉◉◉ ros@ros-pc: ~
ros@ros-pc:~$ lspci
00:00.0 Host bridge: Intel Corporation 440FX - 82441FX PMC [Natoma] (rev 02)
00:01.0 ISA bridge: Intel Corporation 82371SB PIIX3 ISA [Natoma/Triton II]
00:01.1 IDE interface: Intel Corporation 82371AB/EB/MB PIIX4 IDE (rev 01)
00:02.0 VGA compatible controller: InnoTek Systemberatung GmbH VirtualBox Graphi
cs Adapter
00:03.0 Ethernet controller: Intel Corporation 82540EM Gigabit Ethernet Controll
er (rev 02)
00:04.0 System peripheral: InnoTek Systemberatung GmbH VirtualBox Guest Service
00:05.0 Multimedia audio controller: Intel Corporation 82801AA AC'97 Audio Contr
oller (rev 01)
00:06.0 USB controller: Apple Inc. KeyLargo/Intrepid USB
00:07.0 Bridge: Intel Corporation 82371AB/EB/MB PIIX4 ACPI (rev 08)
00:0d.0 SATA controller: Intel Corporation 82801HM/HEM (ICH8M/ICH8M-E) SATA Cont
roller [AHCI mode] (rev 02)
ros@ros-pc:~$ ▮
```

*Figure 1-43.* *Listing the PCI devices*

## lsusb: List of USB Devices in the System

The lsusb command lists all USB devices (see Figure 1-44).

---

Usage: lsusb

---

```
○ ● ○  ros@ros-pc: ~
ros@ros-pc:~$ lsusb
Bus 001 Device 002: ID 80ee:0021 VirtualBox USB Tablet
Bus 001 Device 001: ID 1d6b:0001 Linux Foundation 1.1 root hub
ros@ros-pc:~$
```

*Figure 1-44.*  *Listing the USB devices*

## sudo: Run a Command in Administrative Mode

The sudo command is one of the most important. We use it regularly.
It runs a command with administrative privileges (see Figure 1-45).
We can also completely switch to root (administrator) mode using this
command.

---

Usage: sudo <parameter> <command>

Example: sudo -i

---

This example command switches to root mode.

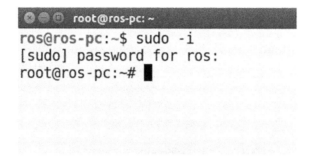

*Figure 1-45.* *Switching to adminstrator mode*

Figure 1-46 shows the results of executing a command in root mode.

```
ros@ros-pc: ~
ros@ros-pc:~$ sudo dmesg
[sudo] password for ros:
[    0.000000] Linux version 4.10.0-28-generic (buildd@lgw01-12) (gcc version 5.
4.0 20160609 (Ubuntu 5.4.0-6ubuntu1~16.04.4) ) #32~16.04.2-Ubuntu SMP Thu Jul 20
 10:19:48 UTC 2017 (Ubuntu 4.10.0-28.32~16.04.2-generic 4.10.17)
[    0.000000] Command line: BOOT_IMAGE=/boot/vmlinuz-4.10.0-28-generic root=UUI
D=fa38abcb-2976-4252-ac26-db79f83f21be ro quiet splash
[    0.000000] KERNEL supported cpus:
[    0.000000]   Intel GenuineIntel
[    0.000000]   AMD AuthenticAMD
[    0.000000]   Centaur CentaurHauls
```

*Figure 1-46.* *Running a command with administrative privilege*

# ps: List the Running Process

The ps command lists the running process in your system.

---

Usage: ps <command arguments>

Example: ps -A

---

When we execute the ps command, it lists the process in the current terminal. If we run ps  -A, it lists all the processes running in the system. Both results are shown in Figure 1-47. PID is the process ID, which identifies the running process. TTY is the terminal type.

```
⊗ ● ◉   ros@ros-pc: ~
ros@ros-pc:~$ ps
  PID TTY          TIME CMD
 2572 pts/2    00:00:00 bash
 2586 pts/2    00:00:00 ps
ros@ros-pc:~$ ps -A
  PID TTY          TIME CMD
    1 ?        00:00:02 systemd
    2 ?        00:00:00 kthreadd
    4 ?        00:00:00 kworker/0:0H
    6 ?        00:00:00 ksoftirqd/0
    7 ?        00:00:00 rcu_sched
    8 ?        00:00:00 rcu_bh
    9 ?        00:00:00 migration/0
   10 ?        00:00:00 lru-add-drain
   11 ?        00:00:00 watchdog/0
```

***Figure 1-47.*** *Listing the processes running on the system*

## kill: Kill a Process

To end a process running in the system, use the kill command.

---

Usage: kill <PID>

Usage: kill 2573

---

To kill a process, we have to identify the PID of process and provide it with the command. The results of the command are shown in Figure 1-48.

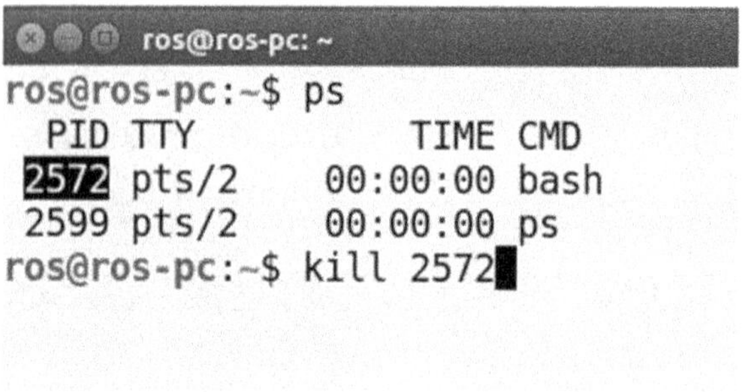

```
ros@ros-pc: ~
ros@ros-pc:~$ ps
  PID TTY              TIME CMD
 2572 pts/2        00:00:00 bash
 2599 pts/2        00:00:00 ps
ros@ros-pc:~$ kill 2572
```

*Figure 1-48.* *Killing a process*

## apt-get: Install a Package in Ubuntu

The apt-get command is important and very useful when working with Ubuntu and ROS. It installs an Ubuntu package that is either in the Ubuntu repositories or on the local system. The packages are called Debian packages, which have .deb extensions. Installing a package requires root permission, so we have to use sudo before the command. We can also update the list of packages in the repositories using this command.

---

Usage: $ sudo apt-get <command_argument> <package_name>

Example: $ sudo apt-get update

Example: $ sudo apt-get install htop

Example: $ sudo apt-get remove htop

---

Figure 1-49 shows the Ubuntu package update using sudo apt-get update. This command updates the package download location in the local system.

```
ros@ros-pc: ~
ros@ros-pc:~$ sudo apt-get update
[sudo] password for ros:
Hit:1 http://in.archive.ubuntu.com/ubuntu xenial InRelease
Get:2 http://security.ubuntu.com/ubuntu xenial-security InRelease [102 kB]
Get:3 http://in.archive.ubuntu.com/ubuntu xenial-updates InRelease [102 kB]
Get:4 http://in.archive.ubuntu.com/ubuntu xenial-backports InRelease [102 kB]
Fetched 306 kB in 3s (80.5 kB/s)
Reading package lists... Done
ros@ros-pc:~$
```

***Figure 1-49.*** *Updating the Ubuntu software repository*

Figure 1-50 shows how to install a package. We are installing a tool called htop. It is a terminal process viewer.

```
ros@ros-pc: ~
ros@ros-pc:~$ sudo apt-get install htop
Reading package lists... Done
Building dependency tree
Reading state information... Done
The following NEW packages will be installed:
  htop
0 upgraded, 1 newly installed, 0 to remove and 149 not upgraded.
Need to get 76.4 kB of archives.
After this operation, 215 kB of additional disk space will be used.
Get:1 http://in.archive.ubuntu.com/ubuntu xenial-updates/universe amd64 htop amd
64 2.0.1-1ubuntu1 [76.4 kB]
Fetched 76.4 kB in 2s (36.1 kB/s)
Selecting previously unselected package htop.
(Reading database ... 175107 files and directories currently installed.)
Preparing to unpack .../htop_2.0.1-1ubuntu1_amd64.deb ...
Unpacking htop (2.0.1-1ubuntu1) ...
Processing triggers for gnome-menus (3.13.3-6ubuntu3.1) ...
Processing triggers for desktop-file-utils (0.22-1ubuntu5.1) ...
Processing triggers for bamfdaemon (0.5.3~bzr0+16.04.20160824-0ubuntu1) ...
Rebuilding /usr/share/applications/bamf-2.index...
Processing triggers for mime-support (3.59ubuntu1) ...
Processing triggers for man-db (2.7.5-1) ...
Setting up htop (2.0.1-1ubuntu1) ...
ros@ros-pc:~$
```

***Figure 1-50.*** *Installing a package on Ubuntu*

The sudo apt-get remove htop command in Figure 1-51 shows how to remove a package. We have to use the remove argument to delete it.

```
ros@ros-pc: ~
ros@ros-pc:~$ sudo apt-get remove htop
Reading package lists... Done
Building dependency tree
Reading state information... Done
The following packages will be REMOVED:
  htop
0 upgraded, 0 newly installed, 1 to remove and 149 not upgraded.
After this operation, 215 kB disk space will be freed.
Do you want to continue? [Y/n] y
(Reading database ... 175115 files and directories currently installed.)
Removing htop (2.0.1-1ubuntu1) ...
Processing triggers for man-db (2.7.5-1) ...
Processing triggers for gnome-menus (3.13.3-6ubuntu3.1) ...
Processing triggers for desktop-file-utils (0.22-1ubuntu5.1) ...
Processing triggers for bamfdaemon (0.5.3~bzr0+16.04.20160824-0ubuntu1) ...
Rebuilding /usr/share/applications/bamf-2.index...
Processing triggers for mime-support (3.59ubuntu1) ...
ros@ros-pc:~$
```

***Figure 1-51.***   *Removing a package from Ubuntu*

Figure 1-52 shows how to install a local Debian package using the apt-get command. The local file is on the same path of the terminal, and the name of the Debian file is htop.deb, so we can use the following:

$ sudo apt-get install ./htop.deb

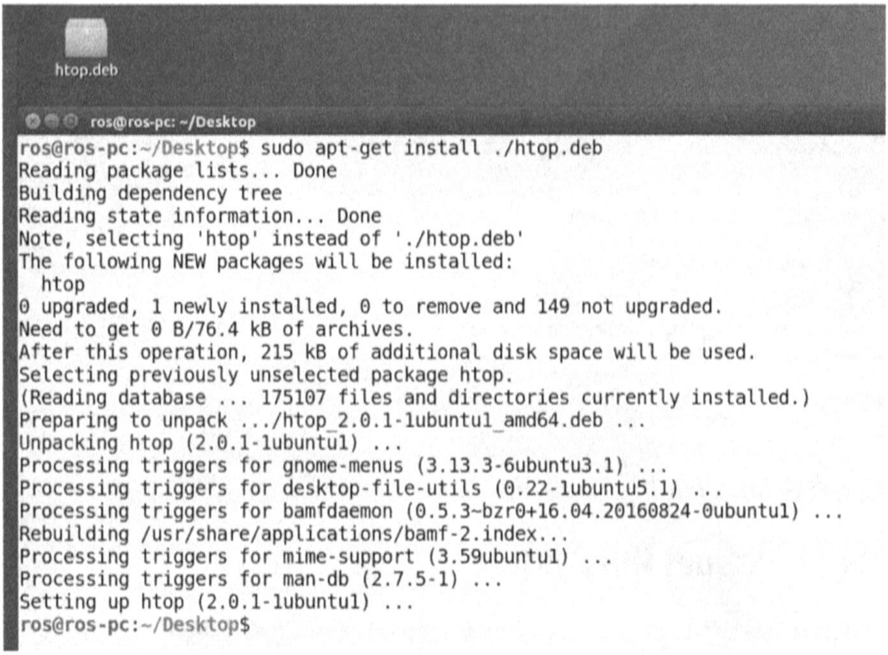

*Figure 1-52.* *Installing a Debian package in Ubuntu*

## dpkg -i: Install a Package in Ubuntu

The dpkg command is another way to install a Debian package.

---

Usage: dpkg <command_arguments> debian file name

Example: dpkg -i htop.deb

---

Figure 1-53 shows the results of the dpkg command.

```
htop.deb

ros@ros-pc: ~/Desktop
ros@ros-pc:~/Desktop$ sudo dpkg -i htop.deb
Selecting previously unselected package htop.
(Reading database ... 175107 files and directories currently installed.)
Preparing to unpack htop.deb ...
Unpacking htop (2.0.1-1ubuntu1) ...
Setting up htop (2.0.1-1ubuntu1) ...
Processing triggers for gnome-menus (3.13.3-6ubuntu3.1) ...
Processing triggers for desktop-file-utils (0.22-1ubuntu5.1) ...
Processing triggers for bamfdaemon (0.5.3~bzr0+16.04.20160824-0ubuntu1) ...
Rebuilding /usr/share/applications/bamf-2.index...
Processing triggers for mime-support (3.59ubuntu1) ...
Processing triggers for man-db (2.7.5-1) ...
ros@ros-pc:~/Desktop$ ▮
```

***Figure 1-53.***  *Installing a Debian package in Ubuntu*

# reboot: Reboot the System

We can restart the system using the terminal command (see Figure 1-54).

---

Usage: `sudo reboot`

---

This instantly reboots the system.

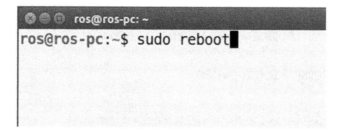

***Figure 1-54.***  *Rebooting PC*

## poweroff: Switch off the System

If you want to instantly shut down the system, use the poweroff command (see Figure 1-55).

---

Usage: $ sudo poweroff

---

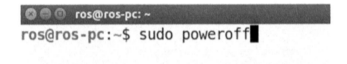

***Figure 1-55.*** *Shutting down the PC*

## htop: Terminal Process View

The htop is a process viewer in Linux (see Figure 1-56). It is not installed in the system by default. You have to install it using apt-get. This command is very useful for managing process.

---

Usage: htop

---

```
  1 [|                                 0.7%]   Tasks: 101, 227 thr; 1 running
  2 [||                                3.9%]   Load average: 0.08 0.22 0.25
  3 [|                                 0.7%]   Uptime: 00:25:00
Mem[|||||||||||||              746M/5.43G]
Swp[                              0K/952M]

  PID USER       PRI  NI  VIRT   RES   SHR S CPU% MEM%   TIME+  Command
 4999 ros         20   0 33104  3840  3192 R  2.0  0.1  0:00.07 htop
    1 root        20   0  181M  6176  4028 S  0.0  0.1  0:02.86 /sbin/init splash
  235 root        20   0 34320  3736  3368 S  0.0  0.1  0:00.26 /lib/systemd/syst
  263 root        20   0 46156  5200  3144 S  0.0  0.1  0:00.36 /lib/systemd/syst
  406 systemd-t   20   0   99M  2576  2356 S  0.0  0.0  0:00.00 /lib/systemd/syst
  379 systemd-t   20   0   99M  2576  2356 S  0.0  0.0  0:00.05 /lib/systemd/syst
  697 root        20   0 28624  3212  2832 S  0.0  0.1  0:00.06 /lib/systemd/syst
  701 root        20   0  4400  1240  1144 S  0.0  0.0  0:00.14 /usr/sbin/acpid
  702 messagebu   20   0 44268  5256  3652 S  0.0  0.1  0:00.58 /usr/bin/dbus-dae
```

***Figure 1-56.*** *Terminal process viewer*

# nano: Text Editor in Terminal

There is a useful text editor that you can use while working in the terminal. You can create code inside the terminal (see Figure 1-57).

---

Usage: $ nano file_name

Example: $ nano test.txt

---

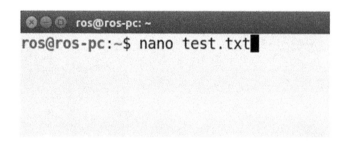

***Figure 1-57.*** *Text editor in the terminal*

Figure 1-58 shows the resulting screen. In this editor, you can enter your code.

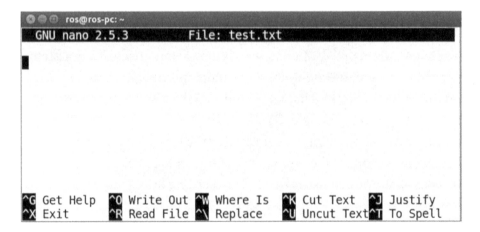

***Figure 1-58.*** *Nano text editor in terminal*

After completing the code, press Ctrl+O to save the file. You are asked to enter the file name. You can enter a new file name or use an existing name. Press Enter to save (see Figure 1-59).

Press Ctrl+X to exit from the editor. To open the file again, use nano file_name.

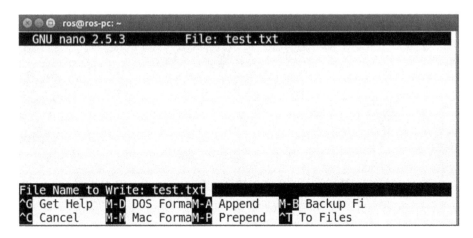

***Figure 1-59.*** *Saving a file in the nano text editor in the terminal*

# Summary

This chapter discussed the fundamentals of the Ubuntu operating system, its installation, and the important shell commands that we need for working with robots. This chapter is important because, before working with ROS-based applications, you should have a basic understanding of Linux and its commands. Understanding the Linux environment and its commands is one of the prerequisites for learning ROS. This book discusses all the prerequisites needed for learning ROS. This chapter is the first step in learning ROS.

# CHAPTER 2

# Fundamentals of C++ for Robotics Programming

In the last chapter, we went through detailed procedures to install Ubuntu on VirtualBox and on a real PC. We also practiced important shell commands that we are going to use while building a robot. The next important requirement for working with a robot is to learn a few programming languages. By using these languages, we can program the robot for different application. Some of the popular programming languages used for creating robotic applications are C++ and Python. This doesn't mean that we won't use other languages. Programming languages like Java and C# are also used in robotics, but the most common languages are C++ and Python.

This chapter discusses some fundamental concepts of C++ and its compilation process. These concepts will definitely help you when you start working with ROS. The fundamentals include mainly object-oriented programming (OOP) concepts and compiling code using Make and CMake tools. This chapter assumes that you have some fundamental understanding of C programming languages. So let's get started with C++ fundamental.

© Lentin Joseph 2018
L. Joseph, *Robot Operating System (ROS) for Absolute Beginners*,
https://doi.org/10.1007/978-1-4842-3405-1_2

# Getting Started with C++

We can define C++ as a superset of the C programming language, or we can say "C with classes." The C++ programming language project, initially called C with Classes, was started in 1979 by computer programmer Bjarne Stroustrup. His main work was adding object-oriented programming into the C language by maintaining its portability without sacrificing speed or low-level functionality. Like C, C++ is a compiled language. It needs a compiler to convert the source code into executable code.

## Timeline: The C++ Language

In 1983, the C with Classes project changed to C++. The ++ operator is used for incrementing a variable, so C++ means it is the C language with new features. In 1990, Borland's Turbo C++ compiler released as a commercial product. In 1998, C++ standards were published as C++ ISO/IEC 14882:1992 or C++98. In 2005, the C++ standards committee released a report of new features added to the latest C++ standard. In 2011, the new C++ standards were completed. The Boost libraries (`www.boost.org`) made a considerable impact on the new standards. Boost C++ Libraries is a set of libraries for the C++ programming that provides support for tasks and structures, such as linear algebra, multithreading, image processing, regular expressions, and unit testing.

# C/C++ in Ubuntu Linux

Ubuntu Linux comes with an in-built C/C++ compiler called GCC/G++. GCC stands for GNU Compiler Collection. It includes compilers for C, C++, Objective-C, Fortran, Ada, and Go, as well as libraries for these languages. GCC was written for the GNU Project (`www.gnu.org/gnu/thegnuproject.html`) by Richard Stallman.

# Introduction to GCC and G++ Compilers

Let's start with GCC/G++ compilers. The latest Ubuntu Linux comes with preinstalled C and C++ compilers. The C compiler in Linux is GCC, and the C++ compiler is G++, the gcc and g++ are shell commands of this compilers. You can type this command in the terminal to see what happens (see Figure 2-1).

```
ros@ros-pc: ~
ros@ros-pc:~$ gcc
gcc: fatal error: no input files
compilation terminated.
ros@ros-pc:~$ g++
g++: fatal error: no input files
compilation terminated.
ros@ros-pc:~$
```

***Figure 2-1.*** *Testing gcc and g++ commands in the terminal*

If you are not getting the message shown in Figure 2-1, then you confirm that these compilers are not preinstalled in your system. No worries! You can install these compilers using apt-get command.

# Installing C/C++ Compiler

First, you may need to update the list of Ubuntu packages from the repository with the following command.

```
$ sudo apt-get update
```

Now install the packages for getting the compilers.

```
$ sudo apt-get install build-essential manpages-dev
```

The build-essential package is associated with numerous packages for developing software in Ubuntu Linux.

# Verifying Installation

After installing the preceding package, you can verify whether the installation is correct by using the following commands.

```
$ whereis gcc
$ whereis g++
```

These commands locate the path of the gcc/g++ command and the manual page of the same command.

The following commands print the GCC compiler that we are going to use and display the path of the command.

```
$ which gcc
$ which g++
```

The following commands print the current version of GCC that we are going to use.

```
$ gcc    version
$ g++    version
```

Figure 2-2 shows the output of the preceding commands.

```
ros@ros-pc: ~
ros@ros-pc:~$ whereis gcc
gcc: /usr/bin/gcc /usr/lib/gcc /usr/share/man/man1/gcc.1.gz
ros@ros-pc:~$ which gcc
/usr/bin/gcc
ros@ros-pc:~$ gcc --version
gcc (Ubuntu 5.4.0-6ubuntu1~16.04.4) 5.4.0 20160609
Copyright (C) 2015 Free Software Foundation, Inc.
This is free software; see the source for copying conditions.  There is NO
warranty; not even for MERCHANTABILITY or FITNESS FOR A PARTICULAR PURPOSE.

ros@ros-pc:~$ whereis g++
g++: /usr/bin/g++ /usr/share/man/man1/g++.1.gz
ros@ros-pc:~$ which g++
/usr/bin/g++
ros@ros-pc:~$ g++ --version
g++ (Ubuntu 5.4.0-6ubuntu1~16.04.4) 5.4.0 20160609
Copyright (C) 2015 Free Software Foundation, Inc.
This is free software; see the source for copying conditions.  There is NO
warranty; not even for MERCHANTABILITY or FITNESS FOR A PARTICULAR PURPOSE.

ros@ros-pc:~$ 
```

***Figure 2-2.*** *Testing gcc and g++ commands in the terminal*

# Introduction to GNU Project Debugger (GDB)

Let's have a look at debugger tools for C/C++. So, what is a debugger?
A debugger is a program that runs and controls another program,
examining each line of code to detect problems or bugs.

The Ubuntu Linux comes with a debugger called GNU Debugger,
which is also called GDB (www.gnu.org/software/gdb/). It is one of the
popular C and C++ program debuggers for the Linux system.

## Installing GDB in Ubuntu Linux

Here is the command to install GDB in Ubuntu. It's already installed on the
latest version of Ubuntu. If you are using other versions, you can use the
following command to install it.

```
$ sudo apt-get install gdb
```

## Verifying Installation

To check whether GDB is installed properly on your PC, use the following command. Once you type **gdb** in your terminal, the message in Figure 2-3 is shown.

```
$ gdb
```

```
ros@ros-pc:~$ gdb
GNU gdb (Ubuntu 7.11.1-0ubuntu1~16.5) 7.11.1
Copyright (C) 2016 Free Software Foundation, Inc.
License GPLv3+: GNU GPL version 3 or later <http://gnu.org/licenses/gpl.html>
This is free software: you are free to change and redistribute it.
There is NO WARRANTY, to the extent permitted by law.  Type "show copying"
and "show warranty" for details.
This GDB was configured as "x86_64-linux-gnu".
Type "show configuration" for configuration details.
For bug reporting instructions, please see:
<http://www.gnu.org/software/gdb/bugs/>.
Find the GDB manual and other documentation resources online at:
<http://www.gnu.org/software/gdb/documentation/>.
For help, type "help".
Type "apropos word" to search for commands related to "word".
(gdb)
```

***Figure 2-3.*** *Testing the gdb command*

You can verify the gdb version by using the following command.

```
$ gdb version
```

The version also shows when you enter the gdb command.

In the next section, we are going to write our first C++ code in Ubuntu. We will compile it and debug it to find bugs in the code.

## Writing Your First Code

Let's start writing the first program in Ubuntu Linux. To write the code, you can use a text editor in Ubuntu. You can choose either the gedit or nano terminal text editor. gedit is a popular GUI text editor in Ubuntu. We already worked with nano in the first chapter, so now let's check out gedit.

In Ubuntu, search for gedit (see Figure 2-4) and select from the search results.

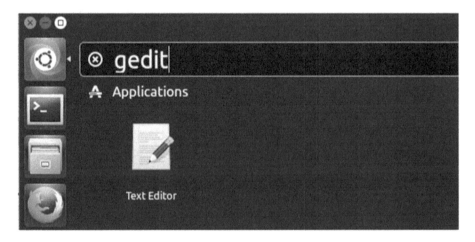

***Figure 2-4.*** *Searching for the gedit text editor in Ubuntu search*

Once you click the text editor, you see the window shown in Figure 2-5.

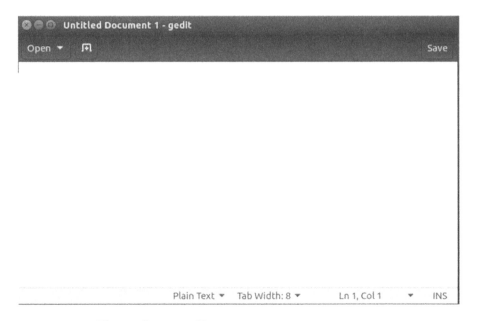

***Figure 2-5.*** *The gedit text editor*

This editor is very similar to Notepad or WordPad in Windows. You can write your first C++ code in this text editor.

Figure 2-6 shows the first C++ code that we are going to compile in the Linux.

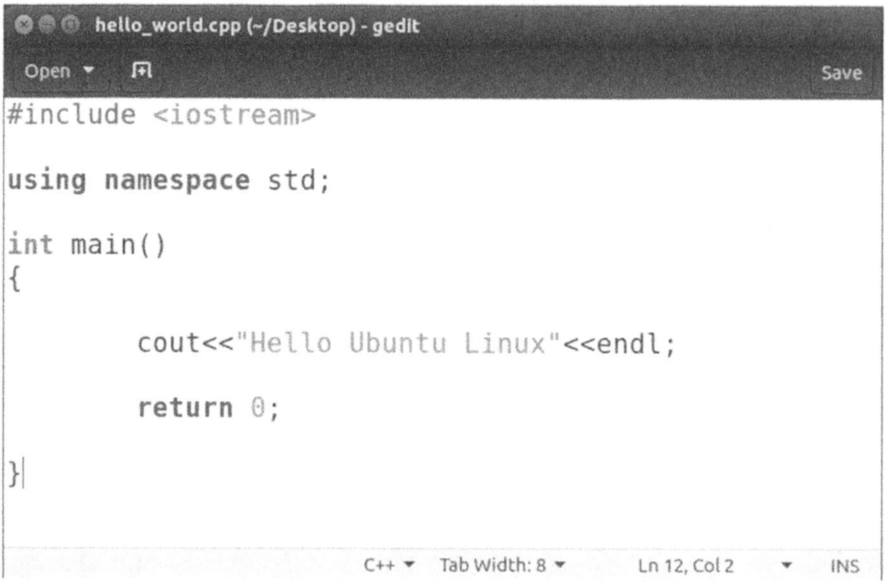

*Figure 2-6.* *The gedit text editor*

Write the code in the text editor and save it as hello_world.cpp.

## Explaining Code

The hello_world.cpp code is going to print the message, "Hello Ubuntu Linux". #include <iostream> is a C++ header file for input/output functions, such as taking input from a keyboard or printing a message. In this program, we are only using the print function to print messages, so iostream will be enough. The next line is using namespace std.

The namespace (www.geeksforgeeks.org/namespace-in-c/) is a special feature in C++ to group a set of entities. The std namespace is used in the iostream library. When we using namespace std, we can access the functions or other entities included in the std namespace, such as functions like cout and cin. If we are not using this line of code, you have to mention std:: for accessing functions inside that namespace; for example, std::cout is a function to print a message.

After discussing the header file and other lines code, we can discuss what is included in the main function. We are using cout<<"Hello Ubuntu Linux"<<endl to print that message. The endl adds a new line after printing the message. After printing the message, the function returns 0 and exits the program.

## Compiling Your Code

After saving your code, the next step is to compile the code. The following procedure will help you to compile the code.

You can take a new terminal and switch the terminal path to the folder where the code is saved. In this case, we have saved the code to /home//Desktop folder. To change the terminal path to the Desktop folder, you have to use the 'cd' command like shown below.

```
$ cd Desktop
```

If you have saved your code in the home directory, you don't need to run this command.

After switching to the Desktop folder, type **ls** to list the files in it (see Figure 2-7).

```
$ ls
```

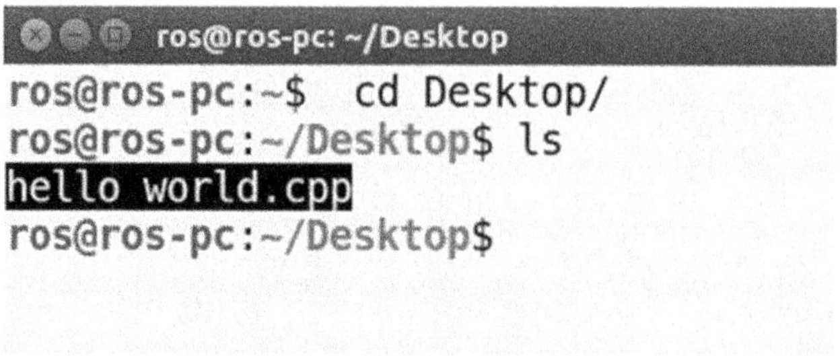

**Figure 2-7.** *Listing the files in the Desktop folder*

If your code is in the folder, you can do the compilation by using the following command.

```
$ g++ hello_world.cpp
```

The G++ compiler checks the code, and if there is no error, it creates an executable named a.out. You can execute this file by using the following command (see Figure 2-8).

```
$ ./a.out
```

It shows the output as

```
Hello Ubuntu Linux
```

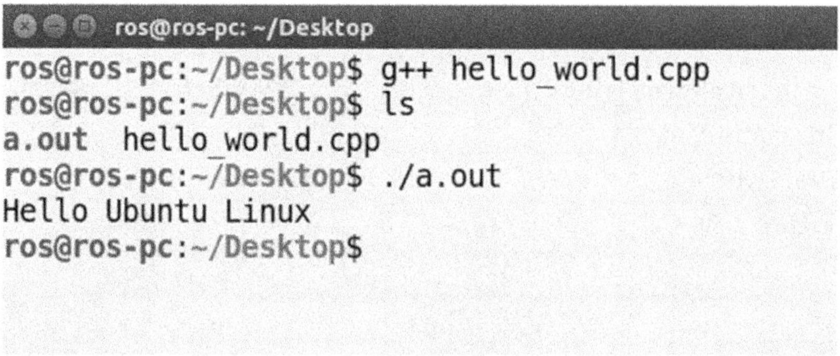

**Figure 2-8.** *Running the output executable*

Congratulations! You have successfully compiled and executed your first C++ code. Now let's check some of the g++ options. This will be useful in the upcoming sections.

If you want to create an executable with a particular name, you can use the following command.

```
$ g++ hello_world.cpp -o hello_world
```

The -o argument points out the output executable name. So, the preceding command creates an executable named hello_world. You can execute it by using the following command.

```
$./hello_world
```

The output of the preceding commands is shown in Figure 2-9.

```
ros@ros-pc: ~/Desktop
ros@ros-pc:~/Desktop$ g++ hello_world.cpp -o hello_world
ros@ros-pc:~/Desktop$
ros@ros-pc:~/Desktop$
ros@ros-pc:~/Desktop$
ros@ros-pc:~/Desktop$ ls
a.out  hello_world  hello_world.cpp
ros@ros-pc:~/Desktop$
ros@ros-pc:~/Desktop$
ros@ros-pc:~/Desktop$
ros@ros-pc:~/Desktop$ ./hello_world
Hello Ubuntu Linux
ros@ros-pc:~/Desktop$
ros@ros-pc:~/Desktop$
ros@ros-pc:~/Desktop$
```

*Figure 2-9.* *Running the hello_world output executable*

## Debugging Your Code

Using the debugger tool, we can go through each line of code and inspect the values of each variable. Figure 2-10 shows C++ code to compute the sum of two variables. Let's save this code as sum.cpp.

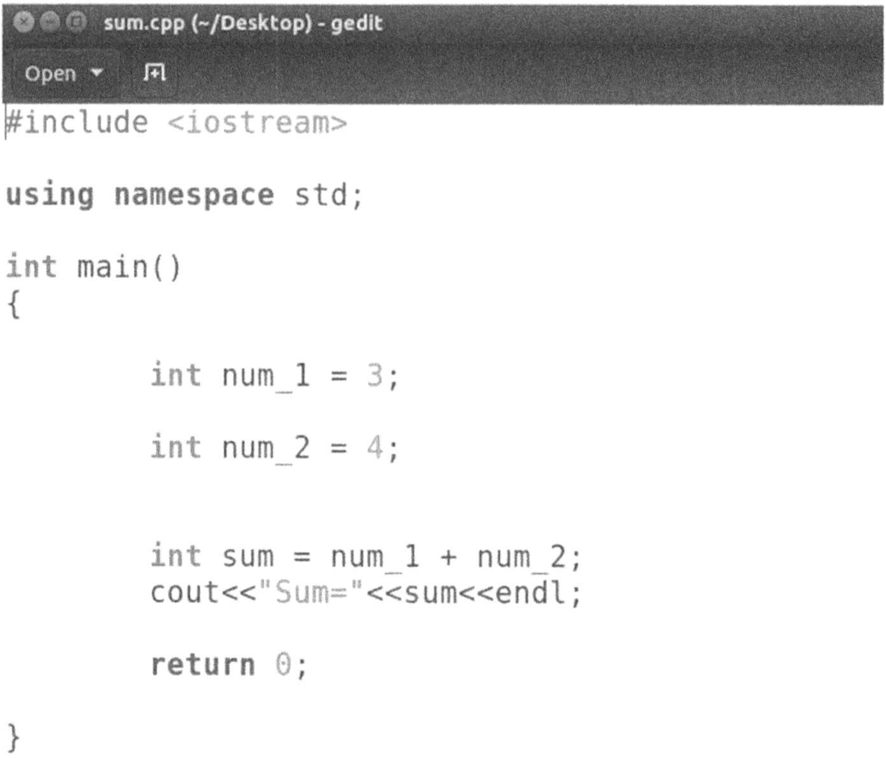

```
sum.cpp (~/Desktop) - gedit

Open ▾    ⊞

#include <iostream>

using namespace std;

int main()
{
        int num_1 = 3;

        int num_2 = 4;


        int sum = num_1 + num_2;
        cout<<"Sum="<<sum<<endl;

        return 0;

}
```

***Figure 2-10.***  *C++ code for summing two numbers*

To debug/inspect each line of code, you have to compile the sum.cpp using g++ with the -g option. This builds the code with debugging symbols and enables it to work with GDB.

The following command helps to compile the code with debug symbols.

```
$ g++ -g sum.cpp -o sum
```

After compiling, you can execute it by running the following command.

```
$. /sum
```

For debugging, use GDB. The output of the preceding set of commands is shown in Figure 2-11.

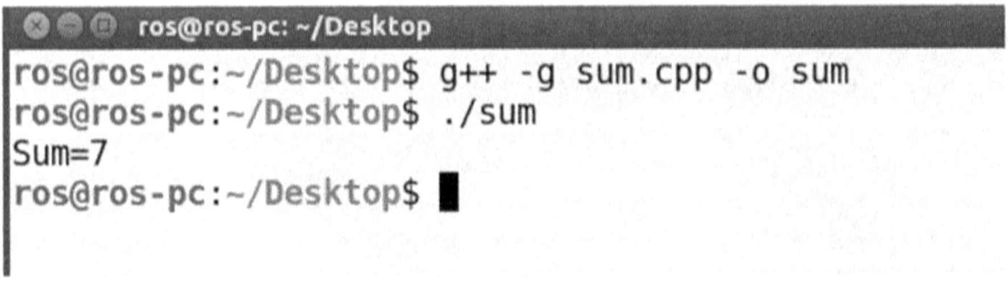

```
ros@ros-pc: ~/Desktop
ros@ros-pc:~/Desktop$ g++ -g sum.cpp -o sum
ros@ros-pc:~/Desktop$ ./sum
Sum=7
ros@ros-pc:~/Desktop$
```

*Figure 2-11.  Compiling sum.cpp*

After creating the executable, you can debug the executable by using following the command.

```
$ gdb sum
```

sum is the name of the executable. After entering the command, you have to use the GDB commands to proceed with debugging. The following are important GDB commands that you need to remember.

- b line_numer: Creates a break point in the given line number. While debugging, the debugger stops at this break point.

- n: Executes the next line of code.

- r: Runs the program until the break point.

- p variable_name: Prints the value of a variable.

- q: Exits the debugger.

Let's try these commands. The output of each command is shown in Figure 2-12.

```
ros@ros-pc: ~/Desktop
ros@ros-pc:~/Desktop$ gdb sum
GNU gdb (Ubuntu 7.11.1-0ubuntu1~16.5) 7.11.1
Copyright (C) 2016 Free Software Foundation, Inc.
License GPLv3+: GNU GPL version 3 or later <http://gnu.org/licens
es/gpl.html>
This is free software: you are free to change and redistribute it
.
There is NO WARRANTY, to the extent permitted by law.  Type "show
 copying"
and "show warranty" for details.
This GDB was configured as "x86_64-linux-gnu".
Type "show configuration" for configuration details.
For bug reporting instructions, please see:
<http://www.gnu.org/software/gdb/bugs/>.
Find the GDB manual and other documentation resources online at:
<http://www.gnu.org/software/gdb/documentation/>.
For help, type "help".
Type "apropos word" to search for commands related to "word"...
Reading symbols from sum...done.
(gdb) b 5
Breakpoint 1 at 0x40089e: file sum.cpp, line 5.
(gdb) r
Starting program: /home/ros/Desktop/sum

Breakpoint 1, main () at sum.cpp:8
8                    int num_1 = 3;
(gdb) n
10                   int num_2 = 4;
(gdb) p num_1
$1 = 3
(gdb) r
The program being debugged has been started already.
Start it from the beginning? (y or n) n
```

***Figure 2-12.*** *Debugging sum application*

Now that you've learned the basics of compiling and debugging, let's start learning the basics of OPP concepts in C++. The following section discusses some of the important concepts that are required knowledge in the upcoming chapters.

# Learning OOP Concepts from Examples

If you already know C structures, then learning about OOP concepts will not take much time. In C structures, we can group different data types— such as integer, float, and string—into a single, user-defined data type. Similar to structures, C++ has an enhanced version of structs that has a provision to define functions. This enhanced struct version is called the C++ class. Each instance of the C++ Class is called an *object*. An object is simply a copy of the actual class. There are several properties associated with objects, which are called *object-oriented programming concepts*. The main OOP concepts are explained with C++ code next.

# The Differences Between Classes and Structs

Before going through the OOP concepts, let's look at the basic differences between a struct and a class. Listing 2-1 helps differentiate them.

***Listing 2-1.***  Example Code to Demonstrate C++ Class and Struct

```
#include <iostream>
#include <string>

using namespace std;

struct Robot_Struct

{
      int id;
      int no_wheels;
      string robot_name;

};

class Robot_Class
{
```

```cpp
public:
        int id;
        int no_wheels;

        string robot_name;

        void move_robot();

        void stop_robot();
};
void Robot_Class::move_robot()
{

        cout<<"Moving Robot"<<endl;

}

void Robot_Class::stop_robot()
{

        cout<<"Stopping Robot"<<endl;
}

int main()

{

        Robot_Struct robot_1;
        Robot_Class robot_2;

        robot_1.id = 2;
        robot_1.robot_name = "Mobile robot";

        robot_2.id = 3;
        robot_2.robot_name = "Humanoid robot";

        cout<<"ID="<<robot_1.id<<"\t"<<"Robot        Name"<<robot_1.
        robot_name<<endl;
```

```
cout<<"ID="<<robot_2.id<<"\t"<<"Robot Name"<<robot_2.
robot_name<<endl;

robot_2.move_robot();
robot_2.stop_robot();

return 0;

}
```

This code defines a struct and a class. The struct name is Robot_Struct and the class name is Robot_Class.

Figure 2-13 shows how to define a structure. It defines a struct with variables such as id, name, and the number of wheels.

```
struct Robot_Struct

{
        int id;
        int no_wheels;
        string robot_name;


};
```

**Figure 2-13.** *Defining a structure in C++*

As you know, a struct has a name, and the declaration of all the variables are inside it. Let's check the definition of a class (see Figure 2-14).

```
class Robot_Class
{

public:
        int id;
        int no_wheels;

        string robot_name;

        void move_robot();

        void stop_robot();

};
```

***Figure 2-14.*** *Defining a Class in C++*

So, what is the difference between the two? A struct can only define a different variables, but a class can define different variables and declare functions too. The class shown in Figure 2-14 declares two functions along with the variables. So where is the definition of each function? We can either define the function inside the class or outside the class. The standard practice is to keep the definition external to the class definition to keep the class definition short.

Figure 2-15 shows the definitions of functions mentioned inside the class.

```
void Robot_Class::move_robot()
{

        cout<<"Moving Robot"<<endl;

}
void Robot_Class::stop_robot()
{

        cout<<"Stopping Robot"<<endl;

}
```

***Figure 2-15.*** *External definition of function inside the class*

In the function definition, the first term is the return data type, followed by the class name, and then the function name followed by ::, which states that the function is inside the class. Inside the function definition, we can add our code. This particular code prints a message.

You have seen the function definition inside a class. The next step is to learn how to read/write to variables and functions.

# C++ Classes and Objects

This section explains how to read/write to structs and classes. Figure 2-16 shows lines of code that do the job.

```
Robot_Struct robot_1;
Robot_Class robot_2;


robot_1.id = 2 ;
robot_1.robot_name = "Mobile robot";


robot_2.id = ;
robot_2.robot_name = "Humanoid robot";
```

***Figure 2-16.*** *Creating struct and class instances*

Similar to the struct instance, we can create an instance of a class and that is called an object.

Let's look at `Robot_Class robot_2`; here, `robot_2` is an object and `robot_1` is an instance of the structure. Using this instance or object, we can access each variable and function. We can use the **.** operator to access each variable. The struct and class variables are accessed by using the **.** operator. If you use struct or class pointers, you have to use the **->** operator to access each variable. Listing 2-2 is an example.

***Listing 2-2.*** Creating a C++ Object and Accessing Object by Reference

```
Robot_Class *robot_2;
robot_2 = new Robot_Class;
robot_2->id - 2;
robot_2->name = "Humanoid Robot";
```

The new operator allocates memory for the C++ object. We can access the functions inside the class and print all values by using the **.** operator. Figure 2-17 shows how to do that.

```
cout<<"ID="<<robot_1.id<<"\t"<<"Robot Name"<<robot_1.robot_name<<endl;

cout<<"ID="<<robot_2.id<<"\t"<<"Robot Name"<<robot_2.robot_name<<endl;

robot_2.move_robot();
robot_2.stop_robot();
```

***Figure 2-17.*** *Printing values and calling functions*

We can save the code as `class_struct.cpp`, and compile it by using the following command.

```
$ g++ class_struct.cpp -o class_struct
$. /class_struct
```

Figure 2-18 shows the output of the code.

```
ros@ros-pc:~$ ./class_struct
ID=2     Robot NameMobile robot
ID=3     Robot NameHumanoid robot
Moving Robot
Stopping Robot
ros@ros-pc:~$ ▉
```

***Figure 2-18.*** *Output of the program*

For further reference, go to www.tutorialspoint.com/cplusplus/ cpp_classes_objects.htm.

# Class Access Modifier

Inside the class, you may have seen a keyword called public:. It is called an *access modifier*. Figure 2-19 is a code snippet of the access modifier used in Listing 2-1.

```
class Robot_Class
{

public:
        int id;
        int no_wheels;
```

***Figure 2-19.*** *Public access keyword usage*

This feature is also called *data hiding*. By setting the access modifier, we can limit the usage of functions defined inside it. There are three types of access modifiers in a class.

- `public`: A public member can access from anywhere outside the class within a program. We can directly access the public variable without even writing functions.

- `private`: Variables or functions cannot be accessed, or even viewed from outside the class. Only the class and friend functions can access private members.

- `protected`: Access is very similar to private members, but the difference is the child class can access the members. The concepts of child class/ derived class are discussed in the upcoming section.

Access modifiers help you group variables, which you can keep visible or hidden in the class.

# C++ Inheritance

Inheritance is another important concept in OOP. If you have two or more classes, and you want to have the functions inside those classes in a new class, you can use the inheritance property. By using the inheritance property, you can reuse the function inside the existing classes in a new class. The new class that is going to inherit an existing class is called a *derived class*. The existing class is called a *base class*.

A class can be inherited through public, protected, or private inheritance. The following explains each type of inheritance.

- *Public inheritance*: When we derive a class from a public base class, the public members of the base class become public members of the derived class, and protected members of the base class become protected members of the derived class. The private members of the base class can never be accessed in the derived class. It can access through calls to the public and protected members of the base class.

- *Protected inheritance*: When we inherit using the protected base class, the public and protected members of the base class become protected members of the derived class.

- *Private inheritance*: When deriving from a private base class, public and protected members of the base class become private members of the derived class.

Listing 2-3 gives a simple example of public inheritance.

***Listing 2-3.*** Example of C++ Public Inheritance

```cpp
#include <iostream>
#include <string>

using namespace std;

class Robot_Class
{

public:
        int id;
        int no_wheels;

        string robot_name;

        void move_robot();

        void stop_robot();

};

class Robot_Class_Derived: public Robot_Class
{

public:

        void turn_left();
```

```cpp
        void turn_right();

};

void Robot_Class::move_robot()
{

        cout<<"Moving Robot"<<endl;

}

void Robot_Class::stop_robot()
{

        cout<<"Stopping Robot"<<endl;
}

void Robot_Class_Derived::turn_left()
{

        cout<<"Robot Turn left"<<endl;

}

void Robot_Class_Derived::turn_right()
{

        cout<<"Robot Turn Right"<<endl;

}

int main()

{

        Robot_Class_Derived robot;

        robot.id = 2;
        robot.robot_name = "Mobile robot";

        cout<<"Robot ID="<<robot.id<<endl;
        cout<<"Robot Name="<<robot.robot_name<<endl;
```

```
    robot.move_robot();
    robot.stop_robot();

    robot.turn_left();
    robot.turn_right();

    return 0;

}
```

So in this example we are creating a new class called Robot_Class_Derived, which is derived from a base class called Robot_Class. The public inheritance is done using a public keyword followed by the base class name (see Figure 2-20). There should be a : after the derived class name, followed by a public keyword and a base class name.

```
class Robot_Class_Derived: public Robot_Class
{

public:

        void turn_left();

        void turn_right();

};
```

***Figure 2-20.*** *Code snippet of public inheritance*

If you chose public inheritance, you can access the public and protected variables and functions of the base class; in this case, Robot_Class.

We are using the same class that we used in the first example. The definition of each function in the derived class is given in Figure 2-21.

```
void Robot_Class_Derived::turn_left()
{

        cout<<"Robot Turn left"<<endl;

}

void Robot_Class_Derived::turn_right()
{

        cout<<"Robot Turn Right"<<endl;

}
```

***Figure 2-21.*** *Function definition inside a derived class*

Now let's look at how to access the functions inside the derived class (see Figure 2-22).

```
        Robot_Class_Derived robot;


        robot.id =  ;
        robot.robot_name = "Mobile robot";

        cout<<"Robot ID="<<robot.id<<endl;
        cout<<"Robot Name="<<robot.robot_name<<endl;

        robot.move_robot();
        robot.stop_robot();

        robot.turn_left();
        robot.turn_right();
```

***Figure 2-22.*** *Accessing the derived class object*

Here we are creating an object of 'Robo_Class_Derived' called 'robot'. If you go through the code, you can understand that we didn't declare id and robot_name variables in the Robo_Class_Derived, but it was defined in the Robo_Class. Using inheritance property, we can access the variable of Robo_Class inside its derived class.

Let's look at the output of the code. We can save this code as class_inherit.cpp and compile it by using the following command.

```
$ g++ class_inherit.cpp -o class_inherit
./class_inherit
```

This gives you the output shown in Figure 2-23, without showing any errors. This means that the public inheritance is working fine.

```
ros@ros-pc:~$ ./class_struct
Robot ID=2
Robot Name=Mobile robot
Moving Robot
Stopping Robot
Robot Turn left
Robot Turn Right
ros@ros-pc:~$
```

***Figure 2-23.***  *Output of a derived class program*

If you look at the output, we are getting all the messages from functions, defined in the base class and the derived class. We can also access the base class variables and set the values.

We have covered some important OOP concepts. To explore more concepts, refer to www.tutorialspoint.com/cplusplus.

# C++ Files and Streams

Let's discuss file operation in C++ and how to read/write data to a file. We have already discussed the iostream header for doing file operations. We need another standard C++ library called fstream. The following three data types are inside fstream.

- ofstream: Stands for *output file stream*. It is used to create a file and to write data into it.

- ifstream: Represents an input file stream. It is used to read data from files.

- fstream: Has both read and write capabilities.

Listing 2-4 demonstrates writing and reading a file using C++ functions.

***Listing 2-4.*** Example C++ Code to Read/Write from a File

```
#include <iostream>
#include <fstream>
#include <string>
using namespace std;
int main()
{
        ofstream out_file;
        string data = "Robot_ID=0";
        cout<<"Write data:"<<data<<endl;
        out_file.open("Config.txt");
        out_file <<data<<endl;
        out_file.close();

        ifstream in_file;
        in_file.open("Config.txt");
        in_file >> data;
```

```
        cout<<"Read data:"<<data<<endl;
        in_file.close();

        return 0;

}
```

We have to include the fstream header to get the read/write data type in C++. We have created an ofstream class object, and in that object, there is a function called open () to open a file. After opening the file, we can write to it by using the << operator. After writing the data, we close the file for a reading operation. For reading, we are using the ifstream class object in C++ and opening the file with the open("file_name") function inside the ifstream class. After opening the file, we can read from the file by using the >> operator. After reading, it is printed on the terminal. The file name that we are going to write is Config.txt and the data is a robot parameter. Figure 2-24 shows the output if we compile the code and run it.

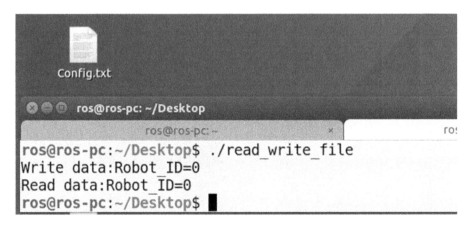

***Figure 2-24.*** *File read/write program*

You can see that Config.txt has been created in the Desktop folder.

For further information, visit www.tutorialspoint.com/cplusplus/cpp_files_streams.htm.

# Namespaces in C++

The namespace concept was mentioned earlier with the Hello World code. In this section, you learn how to create, where to use, and how to access a namespace. Listing 2-5 provides an example of creating and using two namespaces.

***Listing 2-5.*** Example Code for C++ Namespaces

```cpp
#include <iostream>

using namespace std;
namespace robot {
       void process(void)
       {
               cout<<"Processing by Robot"<<endl;
       }
}

namespace machine {
       void process(void)
       {
               cout<<"Processing by Machine"<<endl;
       }
}
int main()
{
       robot::process();
       machine::process();
}
```

To create a namespace, use the namespace keyword followed by name of the namespace. In Listing 2-5, we are defining two namespaces. If you go through the code, you see that the same function is defined inside each namespace. The namespaces are used to group a set of functions or classes that perform a unique action. We can access the members inside the namespace using the name of the namespace followed by :: and the function name. In this code, we are calling two functions inside the namespace, called robot and machine.

Figure 2-25 shows the output of the code in Listing 2-5. The code is saved as namespace.cpp.

```
ros@ros-pc:~/Desktop$ g++ namespace.cpp -o namespace
ros@ros-pc:~/Desktop$ ./namespace
Processing by Robot
Processing by Machine
ros@ros-pc:~/Desktop$ █
```

***Figure 2-25.***  *Output of the namespace code*

For additional reference, visit www.tutorialspoint.com/cplusplus/ cpp_exceptions_handling.htm.

# C++ Exception Handling

Exception handling in C++ is a new method for handling circumstances in which there is an unexpected output in response to user input. The exception can happen during runtime. Listing 2-6 is an example of the C++ exception handling feature.

***Listing 2-6.*** Example of C++ Exception Handling

```cpp
#include <iostream>
using namespace std;
int main()
{
        try
        {
                int no_1 = 1;
                int no_2 = 0;

                if(no_2 == 0)
                {
                        throw no_1;
                }

        }

        catch(int e)

        {
                cout<<"Exception found:"<<e<<endl;
        }

}
```

To handle an exception, we mainly use three keywords.

- try: Inside the try block, we can write our code, which may raise an exception.

- catch: If the try block raises an exception, the catch block catches the exception. We can decide what to do with that exception.

- throw: We can throw an exception from the try
  block when the problem starts to show. If the throw
  statement is executed, it raises an exception and is
  caught by the catch block.

Listing 2-7 shows the general structure.

***Listing 2-7.*** General Structure for Exception Handling

```
try
{
      //Our code snippets
}
catch (Exception name)
{
      //Exception handling block
}
```

The code in Listing 2-6 is checking whether num_2 is 0. If num_2 is 0, an exception is raised by using the throw keyword with num_1, so the catch block can receive the num_1 value for inspecting.

Figure 2-26 shows the output of Listing 2-6.

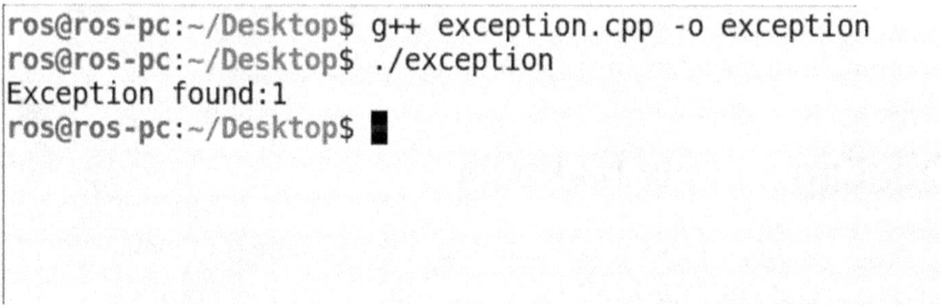

```
ros@ros-pc:~/Desktop$ g++ exception.cpp -o exception
ros@ros-pc:~/Desktop$ ./exception
Exception found:1
ros@ros-pc:~/Desktop$ ▮
```

***Figure 2-26.*** *Output of the exception code*

Inside the catch block, we print the exception value (i.e., the value of num_1, which is 1).

Exception handling is widely using for easily debugging a program.

For further reference, visit `www.geeksforgeeks.org/exception-handling-c/`.

# C++ Standard Template Libraries

If you want to work with data structures such as list, stacks, arrays, and so forth, it is best to look at the Standard Template Library (STL). STL provides the implementation of various standard algorithms in computer science, such as sorting and searching, and data structures like vectors, lists, and queue. This is an advanced C++concept. It is a good idea to review the information at `www.geeksforgeeks.org/the-c-standard-template-library-stl/`.

# Building a C++ Project

Now that you've learned some important OOP concepts, let's have a look at how to build a C++ project. Just imagine, you have hundreds or thousands of lines of source code, and you need to compile and link it. How do you do that? This section discusses that.

If you are working with more than one source code, it is a good idea to review and use the following tools to compile and build your project.

## Creating a Linux Makefile

A Linux makefile is a tool to compile one or more sources in a single command and build the executable. Let's discuss a simple project to demonstrate the makefile capabilities.

We are going to write code for adding two numbers. For the addition, we first create a class. While working with the C++ classes, we write the declaration and definition of the class in the main source code. Another approach is to declare and define the class in a header and .cpp file, and then include this header in the main code for getting that class. This approach is helpful in modularizing the entire project. So, our project has three files.

- main.cpp: The main code that we are going to build.

- add.h: The header file of the add class. It has a declaration of the class.

- add.cpp: This file has the entire definition of the add class.

It is a good idea to use the class name as the name of the header and .cpp file. Here we create the add class so that the name of the header is add.h and add.cpp.

Listing 2-8, Listing 2-9, and Listing 2-10 provide the code for each file.

**Listing 2-8.** add.h

```
#include <iostream>
class add
{
public:
        int compute(int no_1,int no_2);

};
```

**Listing 2-9.** add.cpp

```
#include "add.h"

int add::compute(int a, int b)
{

        return(a+b);

}
```

***Listing 2-10.*** main.cpp

```
#include "add.h"
using namespace std;
int main()
{
        add obj;
        int result = obj.compute(43,34);
        cout<<"The Result:="<<result<<endl;
        return 0;
}
```

In the main.cpp (see Listing 2-10), we include the add.h header file to access the add class. We create an object of the add class, pass two numbers to the compute function, and print the result.

We can compile and execute the code in Listing 2-10 using the following command.

```
$ g++ add.cpp main.cpp -o main
$ ./main
```

The g++ command is easy to use for compiling a single source code, but if we want to compile several source codes, the g++ command is inconvenient. A Linux makefile is one way to compile multiple source codes in a single command. Listing 2-10 shows how to write a makefile for compiling the code.

The code in Listing 2-11 needs to be saved as the makefile.

***Listing 2-11.*** A Linux Makefile

```
CC = g++
CFLAGS = -c
SOURCES =  main.cpp add.cpp
OBJECTS = $(SOURCES:.cpp=.o)
EXECUTABLE = main
```

```
all: $(OBJECTS) $(EXECUTABLE)

$(EXECUTABLE) : $(OBJECTS)
             $(CC) $(OBJECTS) -o $@

.cpp.o: *.h
       $(CC) $(CFLAGS) $< -o $@

clean :
       -rm -f $(OBJECTS) $(EXECUTABLE)

.PHONY: all clean
```

After saving the code in Listing 2-11 as a makefile, you have to execute the following command to build it.

```
$ make
```

This builds the source code, as shown in Figure 2-27.

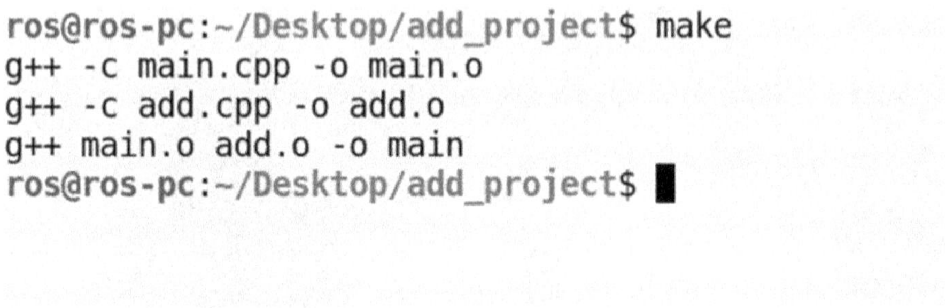

```
ros@ros-pc:~/Desktop/add_project$ make
g++ -c main.cpp -o main.o
g++ -c add.cpp -o add.o
g++ main.o add.o -o main
ros@ros-pc:~/Desktop/add_project$ ▌
```

***Figure 2-27.*** *Output of make command*

After building using the make command, you can execute the program by using the following command. The results are shown in Figure 2-28.

```
$. /main
```

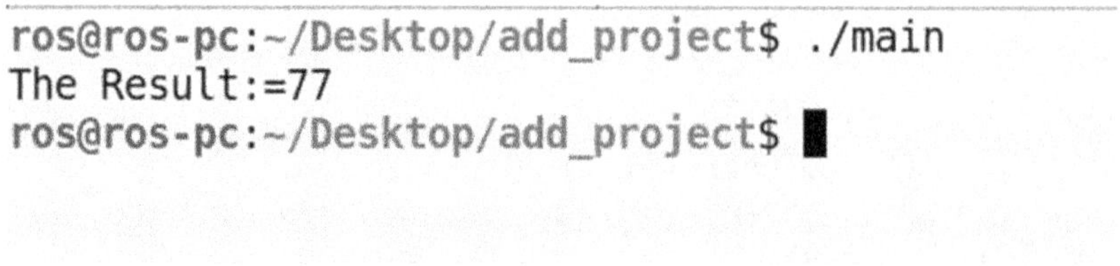

```
ros@ros-pc:~/Desktop/add_project$ ./main
The Result:=77
ros@ros-pc:~/Desktop/add_project$ █
```

*Figure 2-28.*  *Output of main code*

You can learn more about makefiles at www.bogotobogo.com/ cplusplus/gnumake.php.

# Creating a CMake File

CMake (cmake.org) is another approach to building a C++ project. CMake stands for *cross-platform makefile*. It is an open source tool to build, test, and package software across multiple OS platforms.

Install CMake by using the following command.

```
$ sudo apt-get install cmake
```

After installing, you can save Listing 2-12 as CMakeLists.txt.

*Listing 2-12.*  The CMakeLists.txt File

```
cmake_minimum_required(VERSION 3.0)
set(CMAKE_BUILD_TYPE Release)
set(CMAKE_CXX_FLAGS "${CMAKE_CXX_FLAGS} -std=c++14")
project(main)
add_executable(
    main
    add.cpp
    main.cpp
)
```

The code is self-explanatory. It basically sets the C++ flags and creates an executable named main from the source code: add.cpp and main.cpp. The list of CMake commands is available at cmake.org/documentation/.

After saving the preceding commands as CMakeLists.txt, we have to create a folder for building the project. You can choose any name for the folder. Here, we use build for that folder.

```
$ mkdir build
```

After building the folder, switch to the build folder and open the terminal from the build folder.

Execute the following command from the build folder path.

```
$ cmake ..
```

This command parses CMakeLists.txt in the project path. The cmake command can convert CMakeLists.txt to a makefile, and we can build the makefile after that. Basically, it automates the process of making the Linux makefile.

If everything is successful after executing the cmake .. command, you should get the message shown in Figure 2-29.

```
ros@ros-pc:~/Desktop/add_project/build$ cmake ..
-- The C compiler identification is GNU 5.4.0
-- The CXX compiler identification is GNU 5.4.0
-- Check for working C compiler: /usr/bin/cc
-- Check for working C compiler: /usr/bin/cc -- works
-- Detecting C compiler ABI info
-- Detecting C compiler ABI info - done
-- Detecting C compile features
-- Detecting C compile features - done
-- Check for working CXX compiler: /usr/bin/c++
-- Check for working CXX compiler: /usr/bin/c++ -- works
-- Detecting CXX compiler ABI info
-- Detecting CXX compiler ABI info - done
-- Detecting CXX compile features
-- Detecting CXX compile features - done
-- Configuring done
-- Generating done
-- Build files have been written to: /home/ros/Desktop/add_project/build
```

***Figure 2-29.*** *Output of cmake command*

After this, you can make the project by entering the make command ($ make).

If successful, you can execute the project executable ($. /main). Figure 2-30 shows the output of the make command and executable.

```
ros@ros-pc:~/Desktop/add_project/build$ make
Scanning dependencies of target main
[ 33%] Building CXX object CMakeFiles/main.dir/add.cpp.o
[ 66%] Building CXX object CMakeFiles/main.dir/main.cpp.o
[100%] Linking CXX executable main
[100%] Built target main
ros@ros-pc:~/Desktop/add_project/build$ ls
CMakeCache.txt  CMakeFiles  cmake_install.cmake  main  Makefile
ros@ros-pc:~/Desktop/add_project/build$ ./main
The Result:=77
```

***Figure 2-30.***  *Output of the make command and executable*

# Summary

This chapter discussed the fundamentals of the C++ programming language and how to program in the C++ language in Ubuntu Linux. Knowledge of C++ is a prerequisite for working with ROS. The chapter started by discussing the C++ compiler in Ubuntu and how to compile a C++ file using the compiler. After seeing a compilation, we covered Object Oriented Concepts in C++. We discussed the basic difference between C++ classes and structs in C, and important object-oriented programming concepts, such as access modifiers and inheritance. We also saw examples of these concepts. Then we covered file operations, namespaces, exception handling, and the Standard Template Library in C++. The end of the chapter covered how to compile C++ source code using Linux makefiles and CMakeLists.txt files.

In the next chapter, we see how to work with Python in Ubuntu Linux.

# CHAPTER 3

# Fundamentals of Python for Robotics Programming

The last chapter discussed the fundamental concepts of C++ and the object-oriented programming concepts used to program robots. In this chapter, we look at the basics of the Python programming language, which can be used to program robots.

C++ and Python are the common languages used in robotics programming. If your preference is performance, then you should use C++, but if the priority is easiness in programming, you should go with Python. For example, if you are planning to work with a robotic vision application, C++ is a good choice because it can execute the application faster by using less computing resources. At the same time, that application can quickly prototype using Python, but it may take more computing resources. Basically, choosing a programming language for the robotics application is a trade-off between performance and development time.

© Lentin Joseph 2018
L. Joseph, *Robot Operating System (ROS) for Absolute Beginners*,
https://doi.org/10.1007/978-1-4842-3405-1_3

# Getting Started with Python

The Python programming language is a commonly used, general-purpose, high-level, object-oriented programming language popular for writing scripts. When compared with C++, Python is an interpreted language that executes code by line by line. Python was created by Guido van Rossum who started development from 1989, and first internal release was in 1990. It is an open source software managed by the non-profit Python Software Foundation (`www.python.org/psf/`).

The main design philosophy of Python is the readability of code and syntax, which allows programmers to express their concepts in much fewer lines of code.

In robotics applications, Python is commonly preferred where less computation is required, such as writing data to a device using serial communication protocols, logging data from a sensor, creating a user interface, and so forth.

# Timeline: The Python Language

Here are the major milestones in the Python programming language:

- The project started in 1989.

- The first version was released in 1994.

- The second version was released in 2000.

- A popular version of Python, 2.7, was released in 2010.

- The third version was released in 2008.

- The latest version of Python, 3.6, was released in 2016.

# Python in Ubuntu Linux

## Introduction to Python Interpreter

Let's start programming Python in Ubuntu Linux. Like the GNU C/C++ compiler, Python interpreter is preinstalled in Ubuntu. The command shown in Figure 3-1 opens the default Python version interpreter.

```
$ python
```

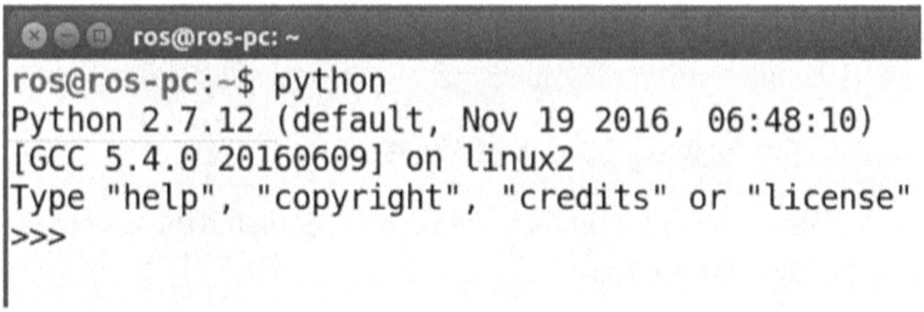

```
ros@ros-pc: ~
ros@ros-pc:~$ python
Python 2.7.12 (default, Nov 19 2016, 06:48:10)
[GCC 5.4.0 20160609] on linux2
Type "help", "copyright", "credits" or "license"
>>>
```

***Figure 3-1.*** *Python interpreter in the terminal*

The default Python version is 2.7.12. You get a list of the installed Python version by pressing the Tab key twice after entering the Python command. The list of Python versions available in Ubuntu are shown in Figure 3-2.

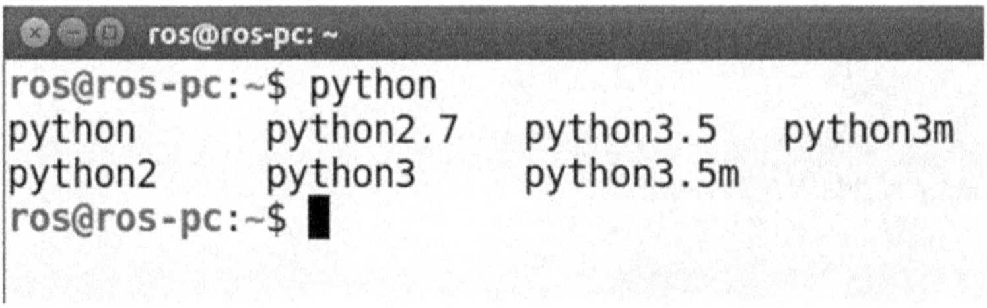

```
ros@ros-pc: ~
ros@ros-pc:~$ python
python        python2.7     python3.5     python3m
python2       python3       python3.5m
ros@ros-pc:~$ █
```

***Figure 3-2.*** *List of Python versions installed on Ubuntu*

Here you see a list of Python commands for two different versions of Python: 2.7.12 and 3.5.2. The python, python2, and python2.7 commands launch version 2.7.12, and the remaining commands launch version 3.5.2. python3m and python3.5m are versions with pymalloc enabled, which performs better for memory allocation than the default memory allocation using malloc (see www.python.org/dev/peps/pep-3149/#proposal).

# Installing Python on Ubuntu 16.04 LTS

As discussed, Python is preinstalled on Ubuntu, but the following command installs Python manually.

**$ sudo apt-get install python python3**

We can also install Python from source code by using the instructions explained in the next section.

# Verifying Python Installation

This section shows how to check the Python executable path and version.

The following checks the current path of the python and python3 commands (also see Figure 3-3).

```
$ which python
$ which python3
```

```
ros@ros-pc:~$ which python
/usr/bin/python
ros@ros-pc:~$ which python3.5
/usr/bin/python3.5
ros@ros-pc:~$
```

***Figure 3-3.*** *Location of Python interpreter*

If you want to see the location of Python binaries, sources, and documentation, use the following command (also see Figure 3-4).

```
$ whereis python
$ whereis python3.5
```

```
ros@ros-pc:~$ whereis python
python: /usr/bin/python2.7 /usr/bin/python /usr/bin/python3
.5 /usr/bin/python3.5m /usr/lib/python2.7 /usr/lib/python3.
5 /etc/python2.7 /etc/python /etc/python3.5 /usr/local/lib/
python2.7 /usr/local/lib/python3.5 /usr/include/python3.5m
/usr/share/python /usr/share/man/man1/python.1.gz
ros@ros-pc:~$ whereis python3.5
python3: /usr/bin/python3 /usr/bin/python3.5 /usr/bin/pytho
n3.5m /usr/lib/python3 /usr/lib/python3.5 /etc/python3 /etc
/python3.5 /usr/local/lib/python3.5 /usr/include/python3.5m
 /usr/share/python3 /usr/share/man/man1/python3.1.gz
ros@ros-pc:~$ ▮
```

***Figure 3-4.*** *Location of Python interpreter, sources, and documentation*

# Writing Your First Code

Our first program will be printing a Hello World message. Let's see how we can achieve it using Python. Before going into the programming, let's look at the two ways in which we can program in Python.

- Programming directly inside Python interpreter
- Writing Python scripts and running using interpreter

These two methods work in the same way. The first method executes line by line inside the interpreter. The scripting method writes all the code in a file and executes using the same interpreter.

The standard practice is to use Python scripting. We may use the Python interpreter shell for testing a few commands.

Let's print a Hello World message in a Python interpreter shell (see Figure 3-5).

```
ros@ros-pc:~$ python
Python 2.7.12 (default, Nov 20 2017, 18:23:56)
[GCC 5.4.0 20160609] on linux2
Type "help", "copyright", "credits" or "license" for more i
nformation.
>>> print 'Hello World'
Hello World
>>>
```

***Figure 3-5.*** *Running Hello World in Python 2.7*

Figure 3-5 shows that it's very easy to print a message in Python. Simply use the print statement along with your message, and press Enter.

### >>> print 'Hello World'

If you are doing the Hello World program in Python version >= 3.0, there are some changes in the Python statement. The main differences are found at https://wiki.python.org/moin/ Python2orPython3. Instead of the print statement used in Python2.x, the following statement is used in Python3.x for printing a message (also see Figure 3-6).

### >>> 'print('Hello World')

```
ros@ros-pc:~$ python3.5
Python 3.5.2 (default, Nov 23 2017, 16:37:01)
[GCC 5.4.0 20160609] on linux
Type "help", "copyright", "credits" or "license" for more i
nformation.
>>> print('Hello World')
Hello World
>>>
```

***Figure 3-6.*** *Running Hello World in Python 3.x*

Let's start scripting using Python. With scripting, we write the code into a file with a .py extension.

The standard way to write Python code is explained at www.python.org/dev/peps/pep-0008/.

We are going to create a file called hello_world.py and write the code in the file (see Figure 3-7). You can use the gedit editor or any text editor for this.

```python
#!/usr/bin/env python
# -*- coding: utf-8 -*-


__author__   = "Lentin Joseph"
__copyright__   = "Copyright 2017, The Hello World Project"
__credits__   = ["Apress"]
__license__   = "GPL"
__version__   = "0.0.1"
__maintainer__   = "Lentin Joseph"
__email__   = "qboticslabs@gmail.com"
__status__   = "Development"


print 'Hello World'
```

*Figure 3-7. The hello_world.py script*

You may be wondering about the purpose of the extra lines in the script when compared to a print statement. There are certain standards to keep in the Python script in order to make it more readable, maintainable, and have all the information about the software that we made.

The first line (#!/usr/bin/env) in Python is called Shebang. If we execute the Python code, the program loader parses this line and executes the reset of the code using that environment. Here we are setting Python as the environment, so the rest of the code will execute in the Python interpreter.

There are coding styles suggested by Google at https://google.github.io/styleguide/pyguide.html.

Let's look at how to execute the preceding code.

# Running Python Code

You can save the hello_world.py in your home folder or in your Desktop folder. If you are in Desktop, you have to switch the path to Desktop.

Figure 3-8 shows the execution of the hello_world.py code.

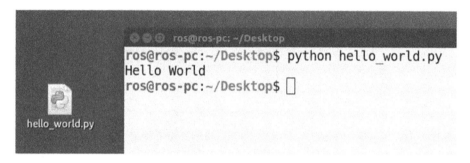

```
ros@ros-pc: ~/Desktop
ros@ros-pc:~/Desktop$ python hello_world.py
Hello World
ros@ros-pc:~/Desktop$ []
```

**Figure 3-8.**  *Executing the hello_world.py script*

Currently, the code is in the Desktop folder, and you can execute the code by using following command.

**$ python hello_world.py**

If your code does not have any errors, it shows output like that shown in Figure 3-8.

There is another way to execute the Python file. Use the following command.

**$ chmod a+x hello_world.py**

By using the chmod command, you are giving executable permission to the given Python code.

You can further explore the chmod command at www.tutorialspoint. com/unix_commands/chmod.htm.

And after giving permission, you can simply execute the Python code using the following command.

**$ ./hello_world.py**

Figure 3-9 shows how to execute the C++ executables too.

```
ros@ros-pc:~/Desktop$ chmod +x hello_world.py
ros@ros-pc:~/Desktop$
ros@ros-pc:~/Desktop$
ros@ros-pc:~/Desktop$ ./hello_world.py
Hello World
ros@ros-pc:~/Desktop$ █
```

***Figure 3-9.*** *Executing the hello_world.py script*

So you have seen how to write a Python script and execute it. Next, we discuss the basics of Python. This is actually a big topic, but we can discuss each aspect of Python by using examples to accelerate learning.

# Understanding Python Basics

The popularity of the Python language is mainly due to its easiness in getting started. The code is short, and we can prototype an algorithm more quickly in Python than in other languages. Because of its popularity, there are a vast number of Python tutorials online. There are active communities to support you. There are extensive libraries to implement your application. The availability of the Python library is one reason to choose this language over others. With a library, you can reduce development time by using existing functions.

Python is a cross-platform language that is widely used in research, networks, graphics, games, machine learning, data science, and robotics. Many companies use this language for automating tasks, so it is relatively easy to get a job in Python.

So how difficult is to learn this language? If you can write pseudo code for a task, then you can code in Python, because it is very similar to pseudo code.

# What's New in Python?

If you know C++, it is easy to learn Python, but you have to be aware of a few things while writing Python code.

## Static and Dynamic Typing

Python is a dynamic typing language, which means that we don't need to provide the data type of a variable during programming; it takes each variable as an object. We can assign any kind of data type to a name. In C++, we have to first assign a variable with a data type, and then we can only assign that type of data to that variable.

C++ is a static typing language; for example, in C++, we can assign like this:

```
int number;

number = 10;   //This will work

number = "10"  // This will not work
```

But in Python, we can assign like this:

```
#No need mention the datatype

number = 10          #This will work
number = "10"        #This will also work
```

So currently, the value of number is "10".

## Code Indentation

Indentation is simply the tab or white space prior to a line of code. In C++, we may use indentation to group a block of code, but it is not mandatory. The C++ code compiles even if we are not keeping any indentation, but it is different in Python. We should keep the block of code in the same indent; otherwise, it shows an indentation error. When indentation is mandatory, the code looks neat and readable.

## Semicolons

In C/C++, semicolons at the end of each statement are mandatory, but in Python, they are not. You can use a semicolon in Python as a separator but not as a terminator; for example, if you want to write a set of code in a line, you can write it by separating semicolons. This can be done in C++ too.

# Python Variables

You have already seen how Python handles variables. Figure 3-10 shows assigning and printing primitive data types, such as int, float, and string. These examples are tested in Python version 2.7.12.

```
>>> number = 10
>>> number_float = 10.3
>>> name = "Lentin"
>>>
>>> print number
10
>>> print number_float
10.3
>>> print name
Lentin
```

***Figure 3-10.*** *Primitive variable handling in Python*

Similar to an array in C/C++, Python provides *lists* and *tuples*. The values inside a list can be access though a list index using square brackets ([ ]); for example, the first element in a list can be accessed by a [0] subscript, which is similar to an array in C/C++.

Figures 3-11 and 3-12 show Python lists and tuples.

```
>>> number_list = [1,2,3,4,5]
>>>
>>> print number_list
[1, 2, 3, 4, 5]
>>>
>>> print number_list[0]
1
>>>
```

***Figure 3-11.*** *Handling lists in Python*

Figure 3-12 shows how we can work with Python tuples.

```
>>> number = ("one","two","three","four")
>>>
>>> print number[0]
one
>>> print number[1]
two
>>> print number[1:]
('two', 'three', 'four')
>>>
```

***Figure 3-12.*** *Handling tuples in Python*

Tuples work similarly to lists, but a tuple is enclosed in parenthesis (()) and a list is enclosed in square brackets ([]). A tuple is a read-only list because its value can't update once it is initialized, but in a list we can update the value.

The next inbuilt data type Python provides is a dictionary. Similar to an actual dictionary, there is a key and a value associated with it. For example, in our dictionary, there is a word and the corresponding meaning of it. The word *here* is the key, and value is its meaning.

Figure 3-13 shows the workings of a Python dictionary.

```
>>> dict = { "one": 1 , "two" : 2 }
>>>
>>> print dict
{'two': 2, 'one': 1}
>>>
>>> print dict.keys()
['two', 'one']
>>>
>>> print dict.values()
[2, 1]
>>>
>>> print dict["one"]
1
```

**Figure 3-13.** *Handling a dictionary in Python*

If we give the key in the dictionary, it returns the value associated with the key.

In the next section, we look at the Python condition statement.

## Python Input and Conditional statement

Similar to C++, Python also has if/else statements to check a condition. In the following example, you see how Python handles user input and makes a decision based on it.

The logic of the program is simple. The program asks the user to enter a command to move a robot. If the user enters a valid command, such as move_left, move_right, move_forward, or move_backward, the program prints that it is moving; otherwise, it prints Invalid command (see Figure 3-14).

```python
#!/usr/bin/env python

robot_command = raw_input("Enter the command:>  ")

if(robot_command == "move_left"):
        print "Robot is moving Left"
elif(robot_command == "move_right"):
        print "Robot is moving right"
elif(robot_command == "move_forward"):
        print "Robot is moving forward"
elif(robot_command == "move_backward"):
        print "Robot is moving backward"
else:
        print "Invalid command"
```

*Figure 3-14. Handling input and the conditional statement in Python*

To take input from a user in Python, we can use either the raw_input() function or the input() function. The raw_input() function accepts any kind of data type, but the input() function only accepts integer types. Here is the syntax of the raw_input() and the input() functions.

```python
var = raw_input("Input message")
var = input("Input message")
```

raw_input() stores the user input in variable called var as a string.

After storing the user input, we compare the input to a list of commands. Here is the syntax for the if/else statement.

```python
if expression1:
    statement(s1)
elif expression2:
    statement(s2)
else:
    statement(s3)
```

A colon ends each expression, after which you have to use indentation for writing the statement. If you don't use indentation, you will get an error.

## Python: Loops

Python has while and for loops, but not do  while loops, by default. Figure 3-15 showcases the usage of the while loop and the for loop in Python. In this example, the robot position in the x and y direction is incremented, and if it is reached in a particular position, the program terminates after printing a message.

```
#!/usr/bin/env python


robot_x = 0.1
robot_y = 0.1

while (robot_x < 2 and robot_y < 2):
        robot_x += 0.1
        robot_y += 0.1

        print "Current Position ",robot_x,robot_y


print "Reached destination"
```

***Figure 3-15.*** *Usage of the while loop in Python*

The following shows the syntax of a while loop.

```
while expression:
        statement(s)
```

In the preceding example, the expression is **(robot_x < 2 and robot_y < 2)**.

There are two conditions inside the expression. We are performing AND logic between two conditions. In Python, 'and', 'or' are logic AND and logic OR.

If the condition is true, the inside statements are executed. As discussed earlier, we have to use proper indents on this block. When, the expression is false, it quits the loop and prints the message 'Destination is reached'.

If we run this code, we get the output shown in Figure 3-16.

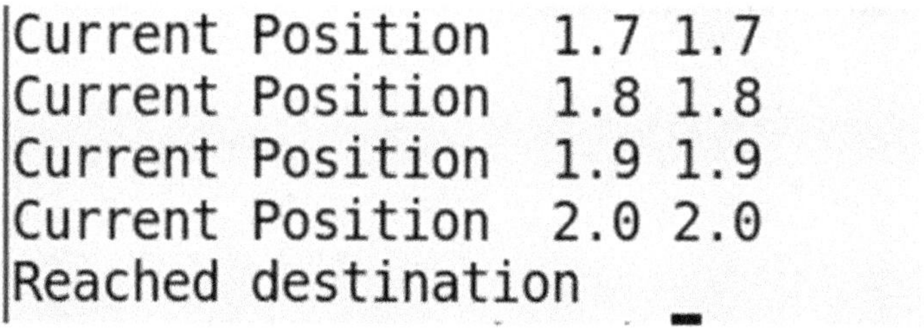

```
Current Position  1.7 1.7
Current Position  1.8 1.8
Current Position  1.9 1.9
Current Position  2.0 2.0
Reached destination
```

***Figure 3-16.***  *Output of the while loop Python code*

We can implement the same application using the for loop in Python. Figure 3-17 shows the workings of the for loop.

```python
#!/usr/bin/env python

robot_x = 0.1
robot_y = 0.1

for i in range(0,100):

    robot_x += 0.1
    robot_y += 0.1

    print "Current Position ",robot_x,robot_y

    if(robot_x > 2 and robot_y > 2):
            print "Reached destination"
            break
```

***Figure 3-17.*** *Python for loop code*

In the preceding code, the for loop executes 0 to 100, increments robot_x and robot_y, and checks if the robot's position is within limits. If the limit is exceeded, it prints the message and breaks the for loop.

The following shows for loop syntax in Python.

```python
for iterating_var in sequence:
    statements(s)
```

Figure 3-18 is the output of the preceding code.

```
Current Position  1.7 1.7
Current Position  1.8 1.8
Current Position  1.9 1.9
Current Position  2.0 2.0
Reached destination
```

***Figure 3-18.*** *Output of python for loop code*

# Python: Functions

As you know, if you want to repeat a block of code with different data, you can write it as a function. Most programming languages have a feature to define a function.

The following is the format to define a function in Python.

```
def function_name(parameter):

    "function_docstring"

    function_code_block
    return [expression]
```

The order of a function definition in Python is important. The function call should be after the function definition. The docstring function is basically a comment with a description of the function and an example of the function's usage. Comments in Python use # on a single line, but if the comment is in a block of code or a docstring, use the following style.

```
'''

<Block of code>

'''
```

Figure 3-19 shows an example of a function in Python.

```python
#!/usr/bin/env python
def forward():
        print "Robot moving forward"
def backward():
        print "Robot moving backward"
def left():
        print "Robot moving left"
def right():
        print "Robot moving right"

def main():
        '''
        This is the main function
        '''

        robot_command = raw_input("Enter the command:>   ")
        if(robot_command == "move_left"):
                left()
        elif(robot_command == "move_right"):
                right()
        elif(robot_command == "move_forward"):
                forward()
        elif(robot_command == "move_backward"):
                backward()
        else:
                print "Invalid command"
if __name__ == "__main__":
        while   :
                main()
```

*Figure 3-19.*  *Example Python code for function*

In Figure 3-19, you can see how to define a function in Python and how to call it. You may be confused with the usage of if __name__ == "__main__". It's basically a common practice, like using int main() in C++. The program also works without this line.

If you enter any of the commands, it calls the appropriate function. The functions are defined at the top of the code. Also note the indentation in each block of code. The function defined in Figure 3-20 does not have any arguments, but you can pass an argument to a function if you want.

```
Enter the command:>  move_forward
Robot moving forward
Enter the command:>  move_backward
Robot moving backward
Enter the command:>  move_right
Robot moving right
Enter the command:>  move_left
Robot moving left
Enter the command:>  move
Invalid command
Enter the command:>  █
```

***Figure 3-20.*** *Output of Python function*

## Python: Handling Exception

An exception is an event that disrupts the normal flow of a program's instruction. When Python encounters a problem, it raises an exception. If we caught an exception, it means the program encountered an error. If the code raises an exception, it can either handle the exception or terminate the program. In this section, we see how to handle an exception in Python.

A simple example of a try-except statement is division by zero. Figure 3-21 shows sample code for try-except.

```
#!/usr/bin/env python

var = input("Enter the number :> ")
try:
        result = 1.0 / var
        print "Result",result

except:
        print "Unable to divide"
```

***Figure 3-21.*** *Example Python try-except*

Whenever the user input is zero, an exception is raised due to division by zero, and that exception is handling statements inside except.

## Python: Classes

This section shows how to write a class in Python. As discussed, Python is an object-oriented programming language like C++. The OOP concepts are the same in both languages. The following is the syntax for a class definition.

```
class ClassName:
        'Optional class documentation string'
        class_suite
```

Here the docstring is an optional component and class_suite has the class members, data attributes, and functions. Class in Python is a vast concept. Let's look at Figure 3-22 as a basic example to get started with classes.

```
#!/usr/bin/env python
class Robot:
        def __init__(self):
                print "Started robot"
        def move_forward(self,distance):
                print "Robot moving forward: "+str(distance)+"m"
        def move_backward(self,distance):
                print "Robot moving backward: "+str(distance)+"m"
        def move_left(self,distance):
                print "Robot moving left: "+str(distance)+"m"
        def move_right(self,distance):
                print "Robot moving right: "+str(distance)+"m"
        def __del__(self):
                print "Robot stopped"
def main():
        obj = Robot()
        obj.move_forward( )
        obj.move_backward( )
        obj.move_left( )
        obj.move_right( )
if __name__ == "__main__":

        main()
```

***Figure 3-22.*** *Python class example*

Figure 3-22 shows an example of moving a robot forward, left, right, and backward. The program simply prints a message; it does not actually move a robot. Let's analyze each part of the program.

The following code is the constructor of the Python class. Whenever we create an object of this class, it executes first. self refers to the current object.

```
def __init__(self):
    print "Started Robot"
```

The following function is the destructor of the class. Whenever an object is destroyed, the destructor is called.

```
def __del__(self):
    print "Robot stopped"
```

We can define methods inside the class, which is how we define it. In all methods, the first argument should be self, which makes the function inside the class. We can pass arguments in a function; in the following example, distance is the argument.

```
def move_forward(self,distance):
    print "Robot moving forward: "+str(distance)+"m"
```

In this function, there are functions to move back, right, and left.

Now let's see how to create an object of the class. The following line creates the object. When an object is created, the constructor of the class is called.

```
obj = Robot()
```

After initializing, we can call each function inside the class by using the following method.

```
obj.move_forward(2)
obj.move_backward(2)
obj.move_left(2)
obj.move_right(2)
```

When the program terminates, the object calls the destructor.

Figure 3-23 shows the output of the preceding example.

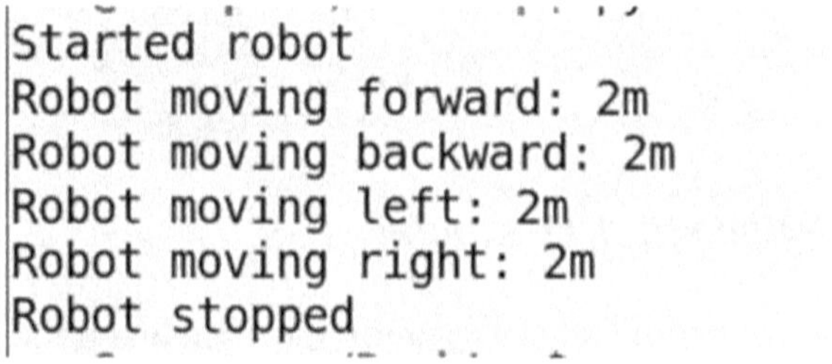

```
Started robot
Robot moving forward: 2m
Robot moving backward: 2m
Robot moving left: 2m
Robot moving right: 2m
Robot stopped
```

***Figure 3-23.***  *Output of Python class example*

In the next section, we learn how to handle files in Python.

## Python: Files

Writing and reading from a file are important in a robotics application. You may have to log data from a sensor, or write a configuration file. This section provides an example program to write and read text to a file in Python(see Figure 3-24).

```python
#!/usr/bin/env python


text = raw_input("Enter the text:> ")
file_obj = open("test.txt","w+")
file_obj.write(text)
file_obj.close()

file_obj = open("test.txt","r")
text = file_obj.readline()
print "Read text: ",text
```

***Figure 3-24.*** *Python file I/O example*

When we run the code, it asks to enter text. The text data saves to a file, and later it reads and prints on the screen. The explanation of Python code is given below.

The following command creates the file handler in reading and writing mode. Like C/C++, there are several file operation modes, such as reading, writing, and appending. In this case, we are using w+ mode, in which we can read/write to a file. If there is an existing file, it is overwritten.

```python
file_obj = open("test.txt","w+")
```

To write to a file, we can use the following command. It writes text into the file.

```python
file_obj.write(text)
```

To close the file, we can use following statement.

```python
file_obj.close()
```

To read the file again, we can use `'r'` mode, like in the following statement.

```
file_obj = open("test.txt",'r')
```

To read a line from a file, we can use `readline()` function.

```
text = file_obj.readline()
```

Figure 3-25 shows the output of the preceding example.

```
Enter the text:> Hello Robot
Read text:  Hello Robot
```

***Figure 3-25.*** *Python file I/O output*

## Python: Modules

C++ uses header files to include a new class or a set of classes. In Python, instead of header files, we use *modules*. A module may contain a class, a function, or variables. We can include the module in our code using the `import` command. The following is the syntax of the `import` statement.

```
import <module_name>
```

```
Example: import os; import sys
```

These are the standard modules in Python.

If there is a list of classes in a module, and we want only a specific class, we can use the following line of code.

```
from <module_name> import <class_name>
```

```
Example: from os import system
```

A module is Python code, but we can create our own modules too. Figure 3-26 shows a test module, which can be imported to our code and execute the function inside it.

```python
#!/usr/bin/env python


class Test:

        def __init__(self):
                print "Object created"

        def execute(self,text):
                print "Input text:> ",text
```

***Figure 3-26.*** *Custom Python test module*

The test.py file has a function called execute() that prints the text passing as a function argument.

A line of code in Python interpreter shows how to use the test module (see Figure 3-27).

```
ros@ros-pc:~/Desktop$ python
Python 2.7.12 (default, Nov 20 2017, 18:23:56)
[GCC 5.4.0 20160609] on linux2
Type "help", "copyright", "credits" or "license" fo
>>>
>>>
>>> import test
>>>
>>> obj = test.Test()
Object created
>>>
>>> obj.execute("Hello")
Input text:>  Hello
>>>
>>>
```

***Figure 3-27.*** *Python test module*

It should be noted that the test.py file should be in the same path as the program or in the Python shell; for example, if test.py is in the Desktop folder, the current path of the shell should also be in the same folder.

When testing, we import the test module by using the import statement. We create object called obj by using following statement.

```
obj = test.Test()
```

This accesses the Test() class inside the test module. After creating the object, we can access the execute() function.

Simple Python tutorials are available at www.tutorialspoint.com/python/.

## Python: Handling Serial Ports

When we build robots, we may have to interface various sensors or microcontroller boards to a laptop or to single board computers such as the Raspberry Pi. Most of the interfacing is through USB or UART communication (https://learn.sparkfun.com/tutorials/serial-communication). Using Python, we can read/write to a serial port on the PC. This helps with reading data from sensors/actuators and writing control commands to the actuators.

Python has a module called PySerial to communicate with the serial port/com port on a PC (https://pythonhosted.org/pyserial/). This module is very easy to use. Let's look at how to read/write to a serial port in Ubuntu using Python.

## Installing PySerial in Ubuntu 16.04

Installing PySerial is a very easy task in Ubuntu. Just follow these commands to install it:

```
$ sudo apt-get update
```

```
$ sudo apt-get install python-serial
```

After installing the module, plug in your serial device; it can be a USB-to-serial device, or an actual serial device. The USB-to-serial device converts the USB protocol to UART protocol. The following are the two most popular USB-to-serial chips available on the market.

- FTDI: `www.ftdichip.com`

- Prolific: `www.prolific.com.tw/US/company.aspx?id=1`

When you plug in the devices with these chips in the Linux based system, it automatically loads the device driver and creates a serial device. The FTDI and Prolific device drivers are available in the Linux kernel. You get the serial device name by executing the `dmesg` command. This command shows the kernel message (also see Figure 3-28).

```
$ dmesg
```

```
[  113.016559] usb 1-5: Product: FT232R USB UART
[  113.016561] usb 1-5: Manufacturer: FTDI
[  113.016563] usb 1-5: SerialNumber: A900fDa9
[  114.043095] usbcore: registered new interface driver usbserial
[  114.043105] usbcore: registered new interface driver usbserial_generic
[  114.043115] usbserial: USB Serial support registered for generic
[  114.044997] usbcore: registered new interface driver ftdi_sio
[  114.045009] usbserial: USB Serial support registered for FTDI USB Serial Device
[  114.045050] ftdi_sio 1-5:1.0: FTDI USB Serial Device converter detected
[  114.045077] usb 1-5: Detected FT232RL
[  114.045219] usb 1-5: FTDI USB Serial Device converter now attached to ttyUSB0
```

***Figure 3-28.*** *Output of dmesg shows the serial device name*

When you plug the serial device to the PC and execute `dmesg`, you see the serial device name. In this case, it is /dev/ttyUSB0.

To communicate with the device, you may have to change the device permission. You can either use `chmod` to change the permission or you can add the current user to the `dialout` group, which gives access to the serial port.

Change the permission of the serial device.

```
$ sudo chmod 777 /dev/ttyUSB0
```

Add a user to the dialout group.

```
$ sudo adduser $USER dialout
```

After doing this, use the code shown in Figure 3-29 to access the serial port.

```
>>> import serial
>>> ser = serial.Serial('/dev/ttyUSB0',9600)
>>>
>>> ser.write('Hello')
5
```

***Figure 3-29.*** *Python example code of writing to a serial port*

In the preceding code, you can see the importing serial module by using the following code.

**import serial**

The following is the command to open the serial port with the given baud rate.

**ser = serial.Serial('/dev/ttyUSB0',9600)**

The following is the command to write to the serial port.

**ser.write('Hello')**

The following is how to read from the serial port.

**text = ser.readline()**

You could also use the following command.

**text = ser.read()**   #This will read 1 byte of data
**text = ser.read(10)**   # read 10 bytes of serial data

The preceding code can interact with Arduino, Raspberry Pi, and other serial sensor devices. You can learn more about Python serial programming at `http://pyserial.readthedocs.io/en/latest/shortintro.html`.

# Python: Scientific Computing and Visualization

In this section, you learn about some of the popular Python libraries for scientific computing and visualization.

- Numpy (`www.numpy.org`): The fundamental package for scientific computing.

- Scipy (`www.scipy.org`): An open source software for mathematics, science, and engineering.

- Matplotlib (`http://matplotlib.org`): A Python 2D plotting library that produces publication-quality figures.

# Python: Machine Learning and Deep Learning

Python is very famous for implementing machine learning and deep learning. The following are the popular libraries in Python.

- TensorFlow (`www.tensorflow.org`): An open source library for numerical computation using data flow graphs.

- Keras (`https://keras.io/`): A high-level, neural networks API that is capable of using TensorFlow, Theano as a back end.

- Caffe (`http://caffe.berkeleyvision.org`): A deep learning framework developed by Berkeley AI Research and community contributors.

- Theano (`http://deeplearning.net/software/theano/`): A Python library that allows you to efficiently define, optimize, and evaluate mathematical expressions involving multidimensional arrays.

- Scikit-learn (`http://scikit-learn.org/`): A simple machine learning library in Python.

## Python: Computer Vision

There are two popular computer vision libraries compatible with Python.

- OpenCV (`https://opencv.org`): Open Source Computer Vision is free for academic and commercial use. It has C++, C, Python, and Java interfaces and supports Windows, Linux, Mac OS, iOS, and Android.

- PIL (`www.pythonware.com/products/pil/`): Python Imaging Library adds image processing capabilities to your Python interpreter.

## Python: Robotics

Python has a good interface for robotics programming using ROS. You can explore more about the capabilities of Python using ROS at `http://wiki.ros.org/rospy`.

## Python: IDEs

There are some popular IDEs (integrated development environments) that make development and debugging faster. The following are three common IDEs.

- PyCharm: `www.jetbrains.com/pycharm/`

- Geany: `www.geany.org`

- Spyder: `https://github.com/spyder-ide`

# Summary

This chapter discussed the fundamentals of Python programming in Ubuntu Linux. Knowledge of Python programming is a prerequisite for working with ROS. We started with the Python interpreter in Ubuntu and saw how to work with it. After working with the interpreter, we saw how to create a Python script and run it on Ubuntu. Then we discussed the fundamentals of Python, such as handling input, output, Python loops, functions, and class operations. After these topics, we saw how to communicate with a serial device using a Python module. At the end of the chapter, we covered Python libraries for scientific computing, machine learning, deep learning, and robotics.

The next chapter discusses the basics of the Robot Operating System and its important technical terms.

# CHAPTER 4

# Kick-Starting Robot Programming Using ROS

The last three chapters discussed the prerequisites for programming a robot using the Robot Operating System (ROS). We discussed the basics of Ubuntu Linux, bash commands, the basic concepts of C++ programming, and the basics of Python programming. In this chapter, we start working with ROS. Before discussing ROS concepts, let's discuss robot programming and how we do it. After this, we learn more about ROS, how to install ROS, and its architecture.

After this, we look at ROS concepts, ROS command tools, and ROS examples to demonstrate ROS capabilities. After that, we discuss the basics of ROS GUI tools and the Gazebo simulator. In the end, we learn how to set up a TurtleBot 3 simulator in ROS.

## What Is Robot Programming?

As you know, a robot is a machine with sensors, actuators (motors), and a computing unit that behaves based on user controls, or it can make its own decisions based on sensors inputs. We can say the brain of the robot is a computing unit. It can be a microcontroller or a PC. The decision making

© Lentin Joseph 2018
L. Joseph, *Robot Operating System (ROS) for Absolute Beginners*,
https://doi.org/10.1007/978-1-4842-3405-1_4

and actions of the robot completely depends on the program running the robot's brain. This program can be firmware running on a microcontroller, or C/C++ or Python code running on a PC or a single board computer, like the Raspberry Pi. Robot programming is the process of making the robot work from writing a program for the robot's brain (i.e., the processing unit).

Figure 4-1 shows a general block diagram of a robot, including the part where it programs.

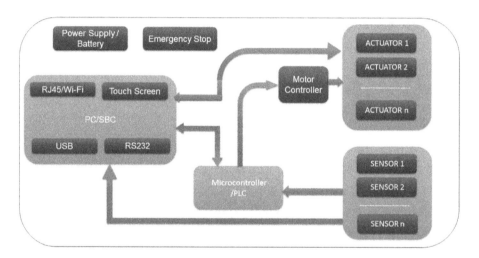

**Figure 4-1.** *General block diagram of a robot*

The main components of any robot are the actuators and the sensors. Actuators move a robot's joints, providing rotary or linear motion. Servo, Stepper, and DC gearmotors are actuator brands. Sensors provide the robot's state and environment. Examples of robot sensors include wheel encoders, ultrasonic sensors, and cameras.

Actuators are controlled by motor controllers and interface with a microcontroller/PLC (programmable logic controller). Some actuators are directly controlled through a PC's USB. Sensors also interface with a microcontroller or PC. Ultrasonic sensors and infrared sensor interface with a microcontroller. High-end sensors like cameras and laser scanners can interface directly with the PC. There is a power supply/battery to power all the robotic components. There is an emergency stop push-button to stop/reset the robot's operation. The two major parts in which to program inside a robot is a PC and a microcontroller/PLC. PLCs are mainly using in industrial robots.

In short, we can say robot programming is programming the PC/SBC and microcontroller/PCL inside robot for performing a specific application using actuators and feedback from various sensors. The robot applications includes pick and place of object, moving robot from A to B. A variety of programming languages can program robots. C/C++, Python, Java, C #, and so forth are used with PCs. Microcontrollers use Embedded C, the Wiring language (based on C++), which is used in Arduino, and Mbed programming (`https://os.mbed.com`). Industrial robot applications use SCADA or vendors' proprietary programming languages, such as ABB and KUKA. This programming is done from the industrial robot's teach pendant. RAPID is the programming language used in ABB industrial robots to automate robotic applications.

Robotic programming creates intelligence in the robot for self-decision making, implementing controllers like PID to move joints, automating repeated tasks, and creating robotic vision applications.

# Why Robot Programming Is Different

Robot programming is a subset of computer programming. Most robots have a "brain" that can make decisions. It can be a microcontroller or a PC. The differences between robot programming and conventional programming are the input and output devices. The input devices include robot sensors, teach pendants, and touch screens, and the output devices include LCD displays and actuators.

Any of the programming languages can program robots, but good community support, performance, and prototyping time make C++ and Python the most commonly used.

The following are some of the features needed for programming a robot.

- *Threading*: As seen in the robot block diagram, there are a number of sensors and actuators in a robot. We may need a multithreaded compatible programming language in order to work with different sensors and actuators in different threads. This is called *multitasking*. Each thread can communicate with each other to exchange data.

- *High-level object-oriented programming*: As you already know, object-oriented programming languages are more modular and code can easily reused. The code maintenance is also easy compared to non-object-oriented programming languages. These qualities create better software for robots.

- *Low-level device control*: The high-level programming langauges can also access low-level devices such as GPIO (general purpose input/output) pins, Serial ports, parallel ports, USB, SPI, and I2C. Programming languages like C/C++ and Python can work with low-level devices, which is why these languages prefer single-board computers like the Raspberry Pi and Odroid.

- *Ease of prototyping*: The easiness in prototyping a robot algorithm is definitely a choice in the selection of programming language. Python is a good choice in prototyping robot algorithms quickly.

- *Interprocess communication*: A robot has lot of sensors and actuators. We can use multithreading architecture or write an independent program for doing each task; for example, one program takes images from a camera and detects a face, another program sends data to an embedded board. These two programs can communicate with each other to exchange data. This feature creates multiple programs instead of a multithreading system. The multithreading system is more complicated than running multiple programs in parallel. Socket programming is an example of interprocess communication.

- *Performance*: If we work with high-bandwidth sensors, such as depth cameras and laser scanners, the computing resources needed to process the data is obviously high. A good programming language can only allocate appropriate computing resource without loading the computing resource. The C++ langauges is a good choice to handle these kind of scenerio.

- *Community support*: When choosing any programming language for robot programming, make sure that there is enough community support for that language, including forums and blogs.

- *Availability of third-party libraries*: The availability of third-party libraries can make our development easy; for example, if we want to do image processing, we can use libraries like OpenCV. If your programming language has OpenCV support, it is easier to do image processing applications.

- *Existing robotics software framework support*: There are existing robotics software frameworks such as ROS to program robots. If your programming language has ROS support, it is easier to prototype a robot application.

# Getting Started with ROS

So far, we have discussed robot programming and how it is different from other computer programming. In this section, we look at a unique software platform for programming robots: the Robot Operating System, or ROS (www.ros.org).

ROS is a free and open source robotics software framework that is used in both commercial and research applications. The ROS framework provides the following robot-programming capabilities.

- *Message passing interface between processes.* ROS provides a message passing interface to communicate between two programs or processes. For example, a camera processes an image and finds coordinates in the image, and then these coordinates are sent to a tracker process. The tracker process does the tracking of the image by using motors. As mentioned, this is one of the features needed to program a robot. It is called *interprocess communication* because two processes are communicating with each other.

- *Operating system–like features.* As the name says, ROS is not a real operating system. It is a meta operating system that provides some operating system functionalities. These functionalities include multithreading, low-level device control, package management, and hardware abstraction. The hardware abstraction layer enables programmers to program a device. The advantage is that we can write code for a sensor that works the same way with different vendors. So, we don't need to rewrite the code when we use a new sensor. Package management helps users organize software in units called *packages*. Each package has source code, configuration files, or data files for a specific task. These packages can be distributed and installed on other computers.

- *High-level programming language support and tools.* The advantage of ROS is that it supports popular programming languages used in robot programming, including C++, Python, and Lisp. There is experimental support for languages such as C #, Java, Node.js, and so forth. The complete list is at `http://wiki.ros.org/Client%20Libraries`. ROS provides client libraries for these languages, meaning the programmer can get ROS functionalities in the languages mentioned. For example, if a user wants to implement an Android application that is using ROS functionality, the rosjava client library can be used. ROS also provides tools to build robotics applications. With these tools, we can build many packages with a single command. This flexibility helps programmers spend less time in creating build systems for their applications.

- *Availability of third-party libraries.* The ROS framework is integrated with most popular third-party libraries; for example, OpenCV (`https://opencv.org`) is integrated for robotic vision, and PCL (`http://pointclouds.org`) is integrated for 3D robot perception. These libraries make ROS stronger, and the programmer can build powerful applications on top of it.

- *Off-the-shelf algorithms.* This is a useful feature. ROS has implemented popular robotics algorithms such as PID (`http://wiki.ros.org/pid`); SLAM (Simultaneous Localization and Mapping) (`http://wiki.ros.org/gmapping`); and path planners such as A*, Dijkstra

133

(http://wiki.ros.org/global_planner), and AMCL
(Adaptive Monte Carlo Localization) (http://wiki.
ros.org/amcl). The list of algorithm implementations
in ROS continuous. The off-the shelf algorithms reduce
development time for prototyping a robot.

- *Ease in prototyping.* One advantage of ROS is off-the-
  shelf algorithms. Along with that, ROS has packages
  that can be easily reused with any robot; for example,
  we can easily prototype our own mobile robot by
  customizing an existing mobile robot package
  available in the ROS repository. We can easily reuse
  the ROS repository because most of the packages
  are open source and reusable for commercial and
  research purposes. So, this can reduce robot software
  development time.

- *Ecosystem/community support.* The main reason for
  the popularity and development of ROS is community
  support. ROS developers are all over the world. They
  actively develop and maintain ROS packages. The
  big community support includes developers asking
  questions related to ROS. ROS Answers is a platform
  for ROS-related queries (https://answers.ros.org/
  questions/). ROS Discourse is an online forum in
  which ROS users discuss various topics and publish
  news related to ROS (https://discourse.ros.org).

- *Extensive tools and simulators.* ROS is built with many
  command-line and GUI tools to debug, visualize,
  and simulate robotics applications. These tools are
  very useful for working with a robot. For example, the
  Rviz (http://wiki.ros.org/rviz) tool is used for

visualization with cameras, laser scanners, inertial measurement units, and so forth. For working with robot simulations, there are simulators such as Gazebo (http://gazebosim.org).

## The ROS Equation

The ROS project can be defined in a single equation, as shown in Figure 4-2.

| | | | |
|---|---|---|---|
| Plumbing | Tools | Capabilities | Ecosystem |

*Figure 4-2.* *The ROS equation*

The plumbing is the same as the message passing interface.
ROS has many other capabilities, which we explore in upcoming sections.

## Robot Programming Before and After ROS

Let's look at the changes to the robotics programming community since the ROS project began.

## The History of ROS

The following are some ROS project historic milestones.

- The ROS project started at Stanford University in 2007, led by roboticist Morgan Quigly (http://people. osrfoundation.org/morgan/). In the beginning it was a group of software developed for robots at Stanford.

- Later in 2007, a robotics research startup called Willow Garage (http://www.willowgarage.com/) took over the project and coined the name ROS, which stands for Robot Operating System.

- In 2009, ROS 0.4 was released, and a working ROS robot called PR2 was developed.

- In 2010, ROS 1.0 was released. Many of its features are still in use.

- In 2010, ROS C Turtle was released.

- In 2011, ROS Diamondback was released.

- In 2011, ROS Electric Emys was released.

- In 2012, ROS Fuerte was released.

- In 2012, ROS Groovy Galapagos was released.

- In 2012, the Open Source Robotics Foundation (OSRF) takes over the ROS project.

- In 2013, ROS Hydro Medusa was released.

- In 2014, ROS Indigo Igloo was released, this was the first long-term support (LTS) release, meaning updates and support is provided for a long period of time (typically five years).

- In 2015, ROS Jade Turtle was released.

- In 2016, ROS Kinetic Kame was released. It is the second LTS version of ROS.

- In 2017, ROS Lunar Loggerhead was released.

- In May 2018, the twelfth version of ROS, Melodic Morenia, was released.

The timeline of the ROS project and a more detailed history is available in at `www.ros.org/history/`.

Each version of ROS is called a ROS distribution. You may be aware of the Linux distribution, such as Ubuntu, Debian, Fedora, and so forth.

Figure 4-3 shows the complete list of ROS distribution releases (`http://wiki.ros.org/Distributions`).

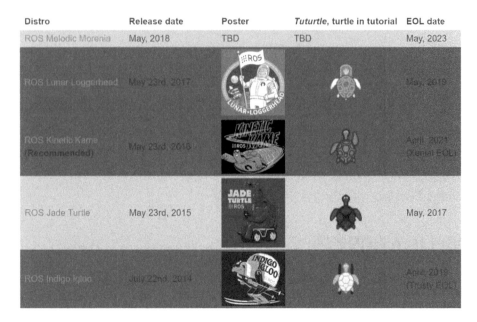

| Distro | Release date | Poster | *Tuturtle*, turtle in tutorial | EOL date |
|---|---|---|---|---|
| ROS Melodic Morenia | May, 2018 | TBD | TBD | May, 2023 |
| ROS Lunar Loggerhead | May 23rd, 2017 | | | May, 2019 |
| ROS Kinetic Kame (Recommended) | May 23rd, 2016 | | | April, 2021 (Xenial EOL) |
| ROS Jade Turtle | May 23rd, 2015 | | | May, 2017 |
| ROS Indigo Igloo | July 22nd, 2014 | | | April, 2019 (Trusty EOL) |

***Figure 4-3.*** *ROS distributions*

If you are looking for the latest ROS features, you can choose new distributions, and if you are looking for stable packages, you can choose LTS. In Figure 4-3, the recommended distribution is ROS Kinetic Kame. In this book, the examples use Kinetic Kame.

ROS is now developed and maintained by the Open Robotics, previously known as the Open Source Robotics Foundation (`www.osrfoundation.org`).

# Before and After ROS

There was active development in robotics before the ROS project, but there was no common platform and community for developing robotics applications. Each developer created software for their own robot, which in most cases, couldn't be reused for any other robot. Developers had to rewrite code from scratch for each robot, which takes a lot of time. Also, most of the code was not actively maintained, so there was no support for the software. Also, developers needed to implement standard algorithms on their own, which took more time to prototype the robot.

After the ROS project, things changed. Now there is a common platform for developing robotics applications. It is free and open source for commercial and research purposes. Off-the-shelf algorithms are readily available, so there is no longer a need to code. There is big community support, which makes development easier. In short, the ROS project changed the face of robotics programming.

# Why Use ROS?

This is common question that developers ask when looking for a platform to program ROS. Although ROS has many features, there are still areas in which ROS can't be used or is not recommended to use. In the case of a self-driving car, for example, we can use ROS to make a prototype, but developers do not recommend ROS to make the actual product. This is due to various issues, such as security, real-time processing, and so forth. ROS may not be a good fit in some areas, but in other areas, ROS is an absolute fit. In corporate robotics research centers and at universities, ROS is an ideal choice for prototyping. And ROS is used in some robotics products after lot of fine-tuning (but not self-driving cars).

A project called ROS 2.0 is developing a much better version of the existing ROS in terms of security and real-time processing (`https://github.com/ros2/ros/wiki`). ROS 2.0 may become a good choice for robotics products in the future.

# Installing ROS

This is an important step in ROS development. Installing ROS on your PC is a straightforward process. Before installing, you should be aware of the various platforms that support ROS.

Figure 4-4 shows various operating systems on which you can install ROS. As discussed, ROS is not an operating system, but it needs a host operating system to work.

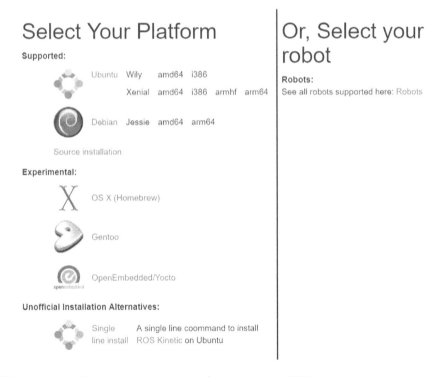

***Figure 4-4.*** *Operating systems that support ROS*

Ubuntu Linux is the most preferred OS for installing ROS. As you can see in Figure 4-4, ROS supports Ubuntu 32-bit, 64-bit, ARM 32-bit, and ARM 64-bit. This means ROS can run on PC/desktops and on single-board

139

computers like Raspberry Pi (http://raspberrypi.org), Odroid (www.hardkernel.com/main/main.php), and NVIDIA TX1/TX2 (www.nvidia.com/en-us/autonomous-machines/embedded-systems/). Debian Linux (www.debian.org) has good ROS support.

In OS X and other operating systems, ROS is still in the experimental phase, which means that ROS functionalities are not yet available.

Let's move on to installation. If you are using a PC or an ARM board running Ubuntu armhf or arm64, you can follow the procedures at http://wiki.ros.org/ROS/Installation.

When you go to this wiki, it asks which ROS version you need to install. Figure 4-5 is a typical website screenshot.

*Figure 4-5.* *Choosing a ROS distribution*

As mentioned, we are choosing ROS Kinetic Kame because it is LTS and stable. If you want to try the latest ROS features, use Lunar Loggerhead.

After you click the distribution that you want, you get the list of operating systems that support that distribution. The list of ROS Kinetic operating systems are shown in Figure 4-4.

Choose the Ubuntu 16.04 (Xenial) operating system. When you select the operating system, you get a set of instructions. The wiki at `http://wiki.ros.org/kinetic/Installation/Ubuntu` provides direct access to instructions for setting ROS in Ubuntu.

We can install ROS in two ways: through a binary installation or by source compilation. The first method is easy and less time-consuming. Binary installation lets you directly install ROS from prebuilt binaries. With source compilation, you create an executable by compiling ROS source code. This takes more time and is based on your PC's specifications.

In this book, we are doing a binary installation.

The following describes the installation steps.

1) *Configure the Ubuntu repositories.* An Ubuntu repository is where the Ubuntu software is organized, typically on servers in which users can access and install the application. There following are repositories in Ubuntu.

   a) Main: Ubuntu officially supported free and open source software

   b) Universe: Community maintained free and open source software

   c) Restricted: This has proprietary device drivers

   d) Multiverse: Software restricted by copyright and legal issues

   To install ROS, we have to enable access to the entire repository so that Ubuntu can retrieve packages from these repositories. Figure 4-6 shows how to do this. Just search in Ubuntu for "Software & Updates".

***Figure 4-6.*** *Searching for the Software & Updates application in Ubuntu*

Figure 4-7 shows that you can enable the access of each repository. You can also select the server location. You can either use a server from your country or the Ubuntu main server.

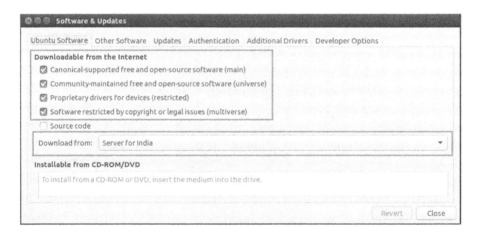

***Figure 4-7.*** *The Software & Updates application in Ubuntu*

OK, you are done with the first step.

2) *Set up your sources.list.* This is an important step in ROS installation. It adds the ROS repository information where the binaries are stored. Ubuntu can fetch the packages after this step is completed. The following is the command used for this.

**Note** Execute the following commands in a terminal.

```
$ sudo sh -c 'echo "deb http://packages.ros.
org/ros/ubuntu $(lsb_release -sc) main" >
/etc/apt/sources.list.d/ros-latest.list'
```

This command creates a new file called /etc/apt/ sources.list.d/ros-latest.list and adds the following line to it.

"deb http://packages.ros.org/ros/ubuntu xenial main".

If we create this file in the sources.list folder and add this line, then only Ubuntu package manager can fetch the package list.

**Note** If you execute $ lsb_release -sc in a terminal, you get the output 'xenial'.

3) *Add the keys.* In Ubuntu, if we want to download a binary or a package, we have to add a secure key in our system to authenticate the downloading process. The package that authenticates using these keys is trusted. The following is the command to add the keys.

```
$ sudo apt-key adv --keyserver hkp://
ha.pool.sks-keyservers.net:80 --recv-key
421C365BD9FF1F717815A3895523BAEEB01FA116
```

4)  *Update the Ubuntu package list.* When we update
    the list, the packages from the ROS repositories also
    list. We use the following command to update the
    Ubuntu repository.

    ```
    $ sudo apt-get update
    ```

5)  *Install ROS Kinetic packages.* After getting the list,
    we download and install the package using the
    following command.

    ```
    $ sudo apt-get install ros-kinetic-desktop-full
    ```

    This command installs all the necessary packages in
    ROS, including tools, simulators, and essential robot
    algorithms. It takes time to download and install all
    these packages.

6)  *Initialize rosdep.* After installing all packages, we
    need to install a tool called rosdep, which is useful
    for installing the dependent packages of a ROS
    package. For example, a typical ROS package may
    have a few dependent packages to work properly.
    rosdep checks whether the dependent packages are
    available, and if not, it automatically installs them.

    The following command installs the rosdep tool.

    ```
    $ sudo rosdep init
    ```

    ```
    $ rosdep update
    ```

7)  *Set the ROS environment.* This is an important step
    after installing ROS. As discussed earlier, ROS comes
    with tools and libraries. To access these command-
    line tools and packages, we have to set up the ROS

environment to access these commands, even though its installed on our system. The following command adds a line in the `.bashrc` file in your home folder, which sets the ROS environment in every new terminal.

```
$ echo "source /opt/ros/kinetic/setup.bash" >> ~/.bashrc
```

Next, enter the following command to add the environment in the current terminal.

```
$ source ~/.bashrc
```

Yes, you are almost done. A small step remains.

8) *Set up dependencies for building the package.* The use of this step can be explained using an example. Imagine that you are working with a robot with more than 100 packages. If you want to set up those packages in a computer, it is difficult to manage all the dependencies needed to install those packages. In that situation, tools like rosinstall are useful. This tool installs all the packages in a single command. In this step, we are literally installing those kinds of tools.

```
$ sudo apt-get install python-rosinstall python-rosinstall-generator python-wstool build-essential
```

Congratulations, you are done with installation. You can verify that your installation is correct by using the following command.

```
$ rosversion -d
```

If you are getting `'kinetic'` as the output, you are all set with the installation.

# Robots and Sensors Supporting ROS

Figure 4-8 shows some of the popular robots that use ROS. A complete list of robots working in ROS is at `http://robots.ros.org`.

The following are the robots shown in Figure 4-8.

   a)  Pepper (`www.ald.softbankrobotics.com/en/ robots/pepper`): A service robot used for assisting people in a variety of ways.

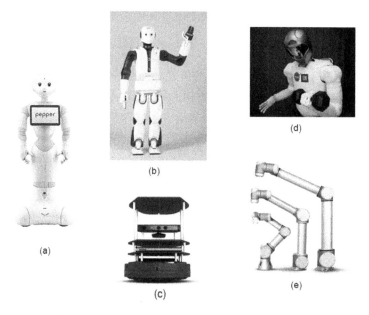

***Figure 4-8.*** *Robots that work in ROS*

   b)  REEM-C (`http://pal-robotics.com/en/products/ reem-c/`): A full-size humanoid robot that is mainly used for research purposes.

   c)  TurtleBot 2 (`www.turtlebot.com/turtlebot2/`): A simple mobile robot platform that is mainly used for research and educational purposes.

d) Robonaut 2 (`https://robonaut.jsc.nasa.gov/R2/`): A NASA robot designed to automate various tasks on the International Space Station.

e) Universal Robot arm: (`www.universal-robots.com/products/ur5-robot`): One of the popular semi-industrial robots widely used for automating various tasks in manufacturing.

There are also sensors supported by ROS. A complete list of these sensors is available at `http://wiki.ros.org/Sensors` (see Figure 4-9).

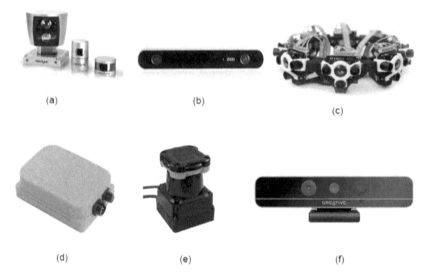

*Figure 4-9.* *Popular sensors that support ROS*

The following describes each sensor shown in Figure 4-9.

a) Velodyne (`http://velodynelidar.com`): Popular LIDARs mainly used in self-driving cars.

b) ZED Camera (`www.stereolabs.com`): A popular stereo depth camera.

c) TeraRanger (www.terabee.com): A new sensor for depth sensing in 2D and 3D.

d) Xsense MTi IMU (www.xsens.com/products/): An accurate IMU solution.

e) Hokuyo Laser (www.hokuyo-aut.jp/): A popular laser scanner.

f) Intel RealSense (https://realsense.intel.com: A 3D depth sensor for robot navigation and mapping.

# Popular ROS Computing Platforms

Figure 4-10 shows a few commonly used ROS-compatible computing platforms.

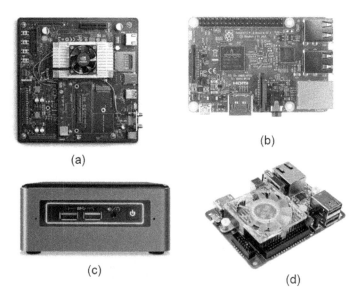

**Figure 4-10.**  *Popular computing units that run ROS*

a)  NVDIA TX1/TX2 (`www.nvidia.com/en-us/
    autonomous-machines/embedded-systems-
    dev-kits-modules/`): Capable of running deep
    learning applications and computational intensive
    applications. The board has an ARM-based 64-bit
    processor that can run Ubuntu. This platform is
    very popular in autonomous robotics applications,
    especially drones.

b)  Raspberry Pi 3 (`www.raspberrypi.org/products/
    raspberry-pi-3-model-b/`): Very popular single-
    board computers for education and research.
    Robotics is a key area.

c)  Intel NUC (`www.intel.com/content/www/us/en/
    products/boards-kits/nuc.html`): Based on a
    x86_64 platform, which is basically a miniature
    version of a desktop computer.

d)  Odroid XU4 (`www.hardkernel.com/main/main.php`):
    The Odroid series boards are similar to Raspberry Pi,
    but it has better configuration and performance. It is
    based on the ARM architecture.

# ROS Architecture and Concepts

We have discussed ROS, its features, and how to install it. In this section
we go deep into ROS architecture and its important concepts. Basically,
ROS is a framework to communicate between two programs or process.
For example if program A wants to send a data to program B, and B wants
to send data to program A, we can easily implement it using ROS. So the
question is whether we implement it using socket programming directly.
Yes, we can, but if we build more and more programs, it gets complex, so
ROS is a good choice for interprocess communication.

Do we really need interprocess communication in a robot? Can we program a robot without it? The answer to the first question is explained in Figure 4-11.

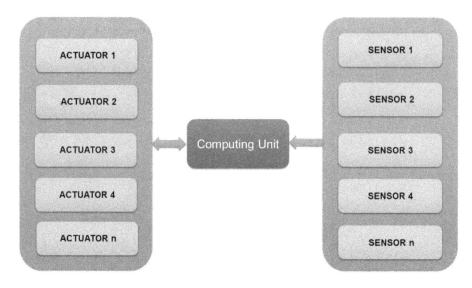

***Figure 4-11.***  *A typical robot block with actuators and sensors*

A robot may have many sensors and actuators, as well as a computing unit. How we can control many actuators and process so much sensor data? Can we do it in a single program? Yes, but that is not a good way of doing it. The better way is, we can write independent programs to handle sensor data and controlling actuators, and often we may need to exchange data between these programs. This is the situation where we use ROS.

So can we program a robot without ROS? Yes, but the complexity of software increases according to the number of actuators and sensors.

Let's see how the communication is happening between two programs in ROS. Figure 4-12 illustrates a basic block diagram of ROS.

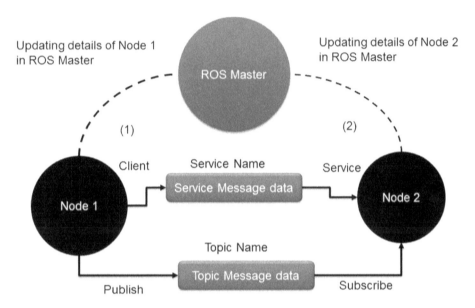

*Figure 4-12.* *ROS Communication block diagram*

Figure 4-12 shows two programs marked as node 1 and node 2. When any of the programs start, a node communicates to a ROS program called the ROS master. The node sends all its information to the ROS master, including the type of data it sends or receives. The nodes that are sending a data are called *publisher nodes*, and the nodes that are receiving data are called *subscriber nodes*. The ROS Master has all the publisher and subscriber information running on computers. If node 1 sends particular data called "A" and the same data is required by node 2, then the ROS master sends the information to the nodes so that they can communicate with each other.

The ROS nodes can send different types of data to each other, which includes primitive data types such as integer, float, string, and so forth. The different data types being sent are called *ROS messages*. With ROS messages, we can send data with a single data type or multiple data with different data types. These messages are sent through a message bus or path called *ROS topics*. Each topics has a name; for example, a topic named "chatter" sends a string message.

When a ROS node publishes a topic, it sends a ROS topic with a ROS message, and it has data with the message type.

In Figure 4-12, the ROS topic is publishing and subscribing node 1 and node 2. This process starts when the ROS master exchange the node details to each other.

Next, let's go through some important concepts and terms that are used when working with ROS. They can be classified as three categories: the ROS file system, ROS computation concepts, and the ROS community.

# The ROS File System

The ROS file system includes packages, meta packages, package manifests, repositories, message types, and services types.

ROS packages are the individual units, or the *atomic units,* of ROS software. All source code, data files, build files, dependencies, and other files are organized in packages. A ROS meta package groups a set of similar packages for a specific application. A ROS meta package does not have any source files or data files. It has the dependencies of similar packages. A ROS meta package organizes a set of packages.

A *package manifest* is an XML file placed inside a ROS package. It has all the primary information of a ROS package, including the name of the package, description, author, dependencies, and so forth. A typical package.xml is shown next.

```
<?xml version="1.0"?>
<package>
  <name>test_pkg</name>
  <version>0.0.1</version>
  <description>The test package</description>

  <maintainer email="qboticslabs@gmail.com">robot</maintainer>

  <license>BSD</license>
```

```
<buildtool_depend>catkin</buildtool_depend>
...............              ............... .

<run_depend>catkin</run_depend>
....... .                    ........... .
```

</package>

A *ROS repository* is a collection of ROS packages that share a common version control system.

A *message type description* is the definition of a new ROS message type. There are existing data types available in ROS that can be directly used for our application, but if we want to create a new ROS message, we can. A new message type can be defined and stored inside the msg folder inside the package.

Similar to message type, a *service type definition* contains our own service definitions. It is stored in the srv folder.

Figure 4-13 shows a typical ROS package folder.

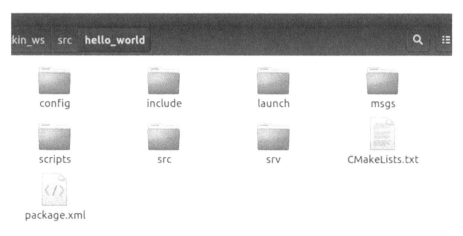

***Figure 4-13.*** *A typical ROS package structure*

# ROS Computation Concepts

These are the terms associated with ROS computation concepts.

- *ROS nodes*: Process that use ROS APIs to perform computations.

- *ROS master*: An intermediate program that connects ROS nodes.

- *ROS parameter server*: A program that normally runs along with the ROS master. The user can store various parameters or values on this server and all the nodes can access it. The user can set privacy of the parameter too. If it is a public parameter, all the nodes have access; if it is private, only a specific node can access the parameter.

- *ROS topics*: Named buses in which ROS nodes can send a message. A node can publish or subscribe any number of topics.

- *ROS message*: The messages are basically going through the topic. There are existing messages based on primitive data types, and users can write their own messages.

- *ROS service*: We have already seen ROS Topics, which is having publishing and subscribing mechanism. The ROS Service has Request/Reply mechanism. A service call is a function, which can call whenever a client node sends a request. The node who create a service call is called Server node and who call the service is called client node.

- *ROS bags*: A useful method to save and play back ROS topics. Also useful for logging the data from a robot to process it later.

# The ROS Community

The following are terms used to exchange ROS software and knowledge.

- The *ROS distribution* is a collection of versioned packages.

- The *ROS wiki* has tutorials on how to set up and program ROS.

- *ROS Answers* (https://answers.ros.org/questions/) has ROS queries and solutions, similar to Stack Overflow.

- *ROS discourse* (https://discourse.ros.org) is a forum in which developers can share news and ask queries related to ROS.

If you want to learn more about ROS concepts, visit http://wiki.ros.org/ROS/Concepts.

# ROS Command Tools

This section discusses ROS command-line tools. What are these tools for? The tools can make our lives easier. There are different ROS tools that we can use to explore various aspects of ROS. We can implement almost all the capabilties of ROS using these tools. The command-line tools are executed in the Linux terminal; like the other commands in Linux, we get the ROS command tools too.

The `roscore` command is a very important tool in ROS. When we run this command in the terminal, it starts the ROS master, the parameter server, and a logging node. We can run any other ROS program/node after running this command. So run roscore on one terminal window, and use another terminal window to enter the next command to run a ROS node. If you run roscore in a terminal, you may get messages like the ones shown in Figure 4-14.

```
roscore http://robot-pc:11311/
robot@robot-pc:~$ roscore
... logging to /home/robot/.ros/log/ac24dafe-0309-11e8-82e3-08
0027c6ff27/roslaunch-robot-pc-4157.log
Checking log directory for disk usage. This may take awhile.
Press Ctrl-C to interrupt
Done checking log file disk usage. Usage is &lt;1GB.

started roslaunch server http://robot-pc:42753/
ros_comm version 1.12.7


SUMMARY
========

PARAMETERS
 * /rosdistro: kinetic
 * /rosversion: 1.12.7

NODES

auto-starting new master
process[master]: started with pid [4168]
ROS_MASTER_URI=http://robot-pc:11311/
```

***Figure 4-14.*** *roscore messages*

You can see messages in the terminal about starting the ROS master. You also see the ROS master address.

The rosnode command explores all the aspects of a ROS node. For example, we can list the number of ROS nodes running on our system. If you type any of the commands, you get complete help for the tool.

The following is a common usage of rosnode.

```
$ rosnode list
```

Figure 4-15 shows the list of nodes running on the system. It is a typical output of rosnode list.

```
robot@robot-pc:~$ rosnode list
/listener
/rosout
/talker
```

***Figure 4-15.***  *Output of a rosnode list command*

The rostopic command provides information about the topics publishing/subscribing in the system. This command is very useful for listing topics, printing topic data, and publishing data.

```
$ rostopic list
```

If there is a topic called /chatter, we can print/echo the topic data using the following command.

```
$ rostopic echo /chatter
```

If we want to publish a topic with data, we can easily do this command.

```
$ rostopic pub topic_name msg_type data
```

The following is an example.

```
$ rostopic pub /hello std_msgs/String "Hello"
```

You can echo the same topic after publishing too. Note that if you run these commands in one terminal, roscore should be running.

Figure 4-16 is a screenshot of rostopic echo and publish.

**Figure 4-16.** *Output of rostopic echo and publish*

Figure 4-16 is the Terminator (`https://launchpad.net/terminator`) application in which the screen is split into separate terminal sessions. One session is running roscore. A second session is publishing a topic. A third session is echoing the same topic.

The `rosversion` command checks your ROS version.

The following command retrieves the current ROS version.

```
$ rosversion -d
Output: kinetic
```

The `rosparam` command gives a list of parameters loaded in the parameter server.

You can use the following command to list the parameters in the system.

```
$ rosparam list
```

Figure 4-17 shows how to set and get a parameter.

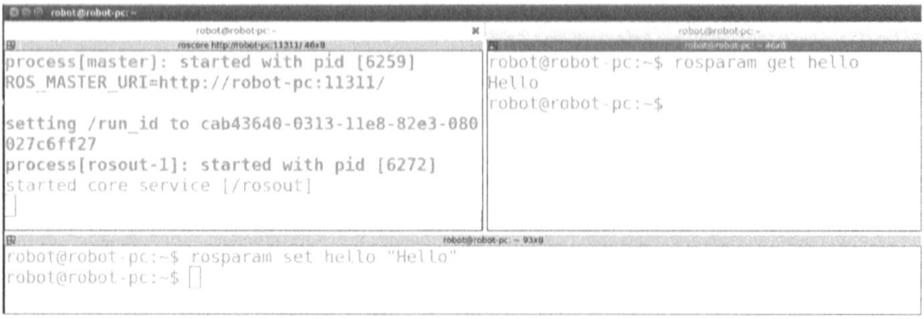

**Figure 4-17.** *Output of rosservice set and get*

You can get the command here.

Setting parameter

```
$ rosparam set parameter_name value
Eg. $ rosparam set hello "Hello"
```

Getting a parameter

```
$ rosparam get parameter_name
$ rosparam get hello
```

Output: "Hello"

The roslaunch command is also useful in ROS. If you want to run more than ten ROS nodes at time, it is very difficult to launch them one by one. In this situation, we can use roslaunch files to avoid this difficulty. ROS launch files are XML files in which you can insert each node that you want to run. Another advantage of the roslaunch command is that the roscore command executes with it, so we don't need to run an additional roscore command for running the nodes.

The following is the syntax for running a roslaunch file. The 'roslaunch' is the command to run a launch file, along with that we have to mention package name and name of launch file.

```
$ roslaunch ros_pkg_name launch_file_name
```

roslaunch roscpp_tutorials talker_listener.launch is an example.

159

To run a ROS node, you have to use the `rosrun` node. Its usage is very simple.

```
$ rosrun ros_pkg_name node_name
```

`rosrun roscpp_tutorials talker` is an example.

## ROS Demo: Hello World Example

This section demonstrates a basic ROS example. The example is already installed in ROS.

There are two nodes: *talker* and *listener*. The talker node publishes a string message. The listener node subscribes it. In this example of the process, the talker publishes a Hello World message and the listener subscribes it and prints it.

Figure 4-18 shows a diagram of the two nodes. As discussed earlier, both nodes need to communicate with the ROS master to get the information from the other node.

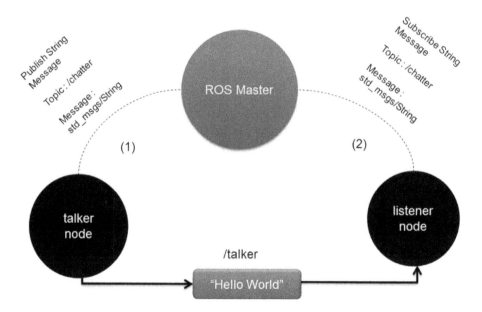

***Figure 4-18.*** *Communication between talker and listener nodes*

Let's start the example by using following command.

The first step in starting any node in ROS is roscore.

```
$ roscore
```

Start the talker node by using the following command in another terminal.

```
$ rosrun roscpp_tutorials talker
```

Now you see the messages printing on the terminal screen. If you list the topic by using the following command, you see a new topic called /chatter.

```
$ rostopic list
```

```
Output: /chatter
```

Now start the listener node by using the following command.

```
$ rosrun roscpp_tutorials listener
```

The subscribing begins between the two nodes (see Figure 4-19).

```
auto-starting new master
process[master]: started with pid [2834]
ROS_MASTER_URI=http://robot-pc:11311/

setting /run_id to 47564656-03b5-11e8-adf0-080027c6ff27
process[rosout-1]: started with pid [2847]
started core service [/rosout]


robot@robot-pc:~$ rosrun roscpp_tutorials talker
[ INFO] [1517093798.629298161]: hello world 0
[ INFO] [1517093798.729495160]: hello world 1
[ INFO] [1517093798.830059323]: hello world 2
[ INFO] [1517093798.929395543]: hello world 3
[ INFO] [1517093799.029379277]: hello world 4
[ INFO] [1517093799.130318738]: hello world 5
[ INFO] [1517093799.229323884]: hello world 6
^Crobot@robot-pc:~$ rosrun roscpp_tutorials listener
[ INFO] [1517093847.208994415]: I heard: [hello world 3]
[ INFO] [1517093847.309478930]: I heard: [hello world 4]
[ INFO] [1517093847.408489287]: I heard: [hello world 5]
[ INFO] [1517093847.508909466]: I heard: [hello world 6]
[ INFO] [1517093847.610700191]: I heard: [hello world 7]
[ INFO] [1517093847.708720524]: I heard: [hello world 8]
```

***Figure 4-19.*** *talker-listener example*

If you want to run two of the nodes together, use the roslaunch command.

```
$ roslaunch roscpp_tutorials talker_listener.launch
```

roscpp_tutorials is an existing package in ROS and talker_
listener.launch.

# ROS Demo: turtlesim

This section demonstrates an interesting application for learning ROS
concepts. The application is called turtlesim, which is a 2D simulator with
a turtle in it. You can move the turtle, read the turtle's current position, and
change the turtle's pattern, and so forth using ROS topics, ROS services,
and parameters. When working with turtlesim, you get a better idea of how
to control a robot using ROS.

The turtlesim application is already installed on ROS. You can start this application by using the following commands.

Starting roscore

$ roscore

Starting Turtlesim application

$ rosrun turtlesim turtlesim_node

A screen like the one shown in Figure 4-20 means that everything is working fine.

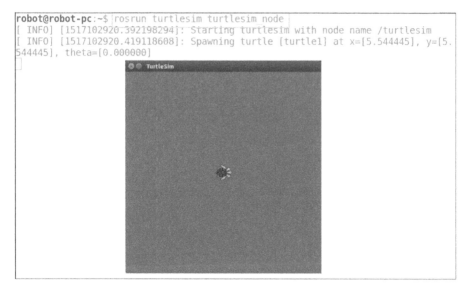

***Figure 4-20.*** *Turtlesim*

Now you can open a new terminal and list the topics by publishing the turtlesim node.

$ rostopic list

You see the topics shown in Figure 4-21.

```
robot@robot-pc:~$ rostopic list
/rosout
/rosout_agg
/turtle1/cmd_vel
/turtle1/color_sensor
/turtle1/pose
```

*Figure 4-21.* *Turtlesim topics*

Figure 4-22 lists the services created by the turtlesim node. You can list the services by using the following command.

```
$ rosservice list
```

```
robot@robot-pc:~$ rosservice list
/clear
/kill
/reset
/rosout/get_loggers
/rosout/set_logger_level
/spawn
/turtle1/set_pen
/turtle1/teleport_absolute
/turtle1/teleport_relative
/turtlesim/get_loggers
/turtlesim/set_logger_level
```

*Figure 4-22.* *List of ROS services*

List the ROS parameters by using the following command (see Figure 4-23).

```
$ rosparam list
```

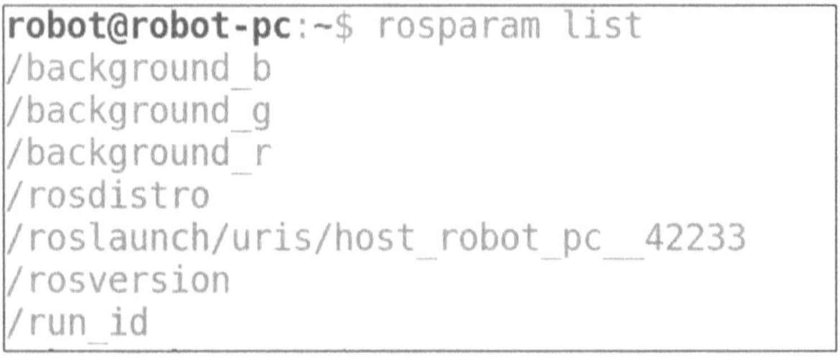

```
robot@robot-pc:~$ rosparam list
/background_b
/background_g
/background_r
/rosdistro
/roslaunch/uris/host_robot_pc__42233
/rosversion
/run_id
```

**Figure 4-23.** *List of ROS parameters*

## Moving the Turtle

If you want to move the turtle, start another ROS node by using the following command. This command has to start in another terminal.

```
$ rosrun turtlesim turtle_teleop_key
```

You can control the robot using your keyboard's arrow keys. When you press an arrow key, it publishes velocity to /turtle1/cmd_vel, which makes the turtle move (see Figure 4-24).

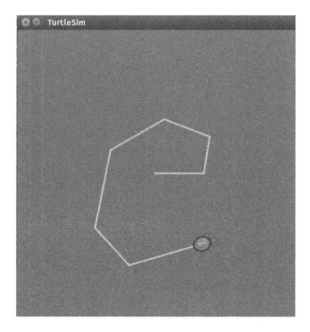

***Figure 4-24.*** *The path that the turtle covers*

If you want to see the back end of these nodes, check the diagram in Figure 4-25. It shows the topic data going to turtlesim.

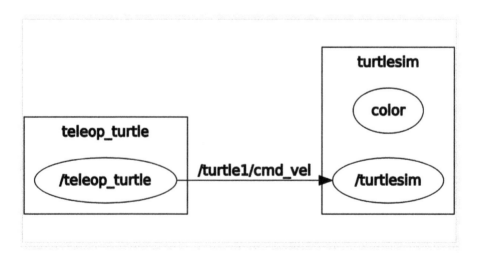

***Figure 4-25.*** *Turtlesim and teleop node back ends*

## Moving the Turtle in a Square

This section shows how to move the turtle along a square path. Close all the running nodes by pressing Ctrl+C, and start a new turtlesim session using the following command (see Figure 4-26).

```
Starting roscore
$ roscore
```

```
Starting turtlesim node
$ rosrun turtlesim turtlesim_node
```

```
Starting the node for drawing square
$ rosrun turtlesim draw_square
```

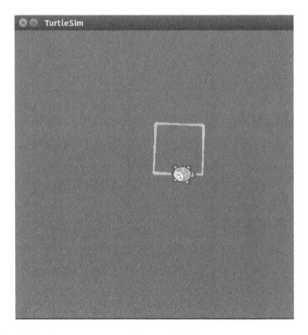

***Figure 4-26.*** *The draw square in turtlesim*

If we want to clear the turtlesim, we can call a service called /reset.

```
$ rosservice call /reset
```

This resets the turtle's position.

In the next section, we look at ROS GUI tools.

# ROS GUI Tools: Rviz and Rqt

Along with command-line tools, ROS has GUI tools to visualize sensor data. A popular GUI tool is Rviz (see Figure 4-27). Using Rviz, we can visualize image data, 3D point clouds, and robot models, as well as transform data and so forth. This section explores the basics of the Rviz tool, which comes with the ROS installation.

Start Rviz using following the command.

Start roscore

```
$ roscore
```

Start rviz

```
$ rosrun rviz rviz
```

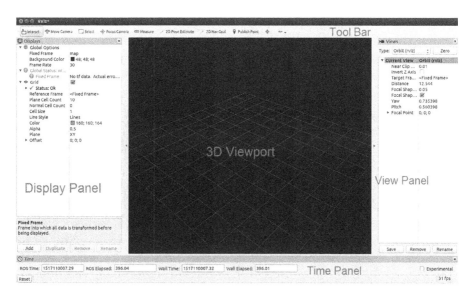

***Figure 4-27.*** *Rviz*

The following describes sections in Rviz.

- *3D viewport*: The area to visualize the 3D data from sensors, robot transform data, 3D model data, and other kinds of 3D information.

- *Display panel*: Displays various kinds of sensor data.

- *View panel*: Options to view the 3D view port according to the application.

- *Toolbar*: Options for interacting with the 3D viewport, measuring robot position, setting the robot navigation goal, and changing camera view.

- *Time panel*: Features information about the ROS time and elapsed time. This time stamping may be useful for processing the sensor data.

- *Rqt*: Features options to visualize 2D data, logging topics, publishing topics, calling services, and more.

This is how to start the Rqt GUI.

Start roscore

```
$ roscore
```

Start rqt_gui
```
$ rosrun rqt_gui rqt_gui
```

You get an empty GUI with some menus. You can add your own plug-ins from the drop-down menu. Figure 4-28 is a screenshot of rqt_gui loaded with a plug-in.

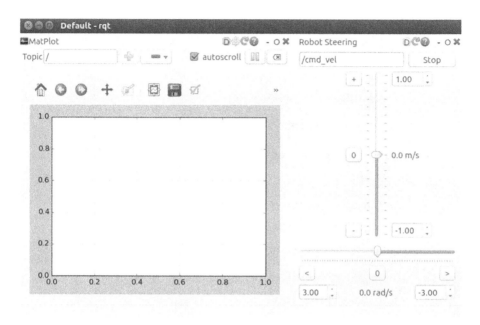

**Figure 4-28.** *The Rqt GUI*

# Summary

This chapter discussed the fundamentals of the Robot Operating System. It started with robot programming and explained why it is different from other software applications. Next, we looked at the different operating system platforms that can install ROS and covered the detailed installation instructions for Ubuntu. We saw different robots and sensors compatible with ROS, and we discussed the ROS architecture. We also looked at important ROS concepts and a simulator called turtlesim. In the end, we became familiar with ROS GUI tools such as Rqt and Rviz.

In the next chapter, we see how to program using ROS and how to create ROS applications using C++ and Python.

# CHAPTER 5

# Programming with ROS

The previous chapter discussed the basics of the Robot Operating System, and in this chapter, you are going to program using ROS. The main programming languages that we are going to use are C++ and Python. We already discussed the basics of C++ and Python in Chapter 2 and Chapter 3. Those fundamental concepts can be applied here to start working with ROS. You will see examples in Python and in C++, so you get a fundamental idea about both languages.

The chapter covers creating a ROS workspace, ROS package and ROS nodes. After creating the package and basic ROS nodes, you will see how to program the turtlesim simulator from the previous chapter. Next, you are introduced to the Gazebo simulator and TurtleBot robot simulation, creating basic ROS nodes to move the TurtleBot in the simulation. Afterward, you learn how to interface and program an Arduino and Tiva-C Launchpad using ROS. These tutorials are very useful for when we create our own robot. At the end of the chapter, you see how to set up ROS and program it in the Raspberry Pi 3.

## Programming Using ROS

We have already covered basic programming using C++ and Python. What does programming with ROS mean? It means that ROS provides some built-in functions to implement ROS capabilities. For example, if we want

© Lentin Joseph 2018
L. Joseph, *Robot Operating System (ROS) for Absolute Beginners*,
https://doi.org/10.1007/978-1-4842-3405-1_5

to implement a new ROS topic, or a new ROS message, or a ROS service, we can simply call these ROS built-in functions to create it. We don't need to implement ROS features from scratch. The programs that use ROS built-in functions/APIs (application program interface) are called *ROS nodes*.

In this chapter, we create ROS nodes for different applications. The ROS wiki provides extensive documentation on creating ROS nodes. As a beginner, it may be difficult to understand most of the topics mentioned on the ROS wiki. This chapter gives you a brief look at them to get started with ROS programming.

There are some steps that we need to take before proceeding to ROS programming. The first step is to create a ROS workspace. The next section discusses the ROS workspace and how to create it.

# Creating a ROS Workspace and Package

The first step in ROS development is the creation of the ROS workspace, which is where ROS packages are kept. We can create new packages, install existing packages, build and create new executables.

You must first create a ROS workspace folder. You can give it any name, and you can create it in any location. Normally, this is in the Ubuntu home folder.

At a new terminal, enter the following command. This creates a folder called catkin_ws, inside of which is another folder called src. The ROS workspace is also called the *catkin workspace*. You see more of catkin in the next section.

```
$ mkdir -p ~/catkin_ws/src
```

The name of the src folder shouldn't be changed. You can change the workspace folder name, however.

After entering the command, switch to the src folder by using the cd command.

```
$ cd catkin_ws/src
```

The following command initializes a new ROS workspace. If you are not initializing a workspace, you cannot create and build the packages properly.

```
$ catkin_init_workspace
```

After this command, you should see the message in Figure 5-1 on your terminal.

```
robot@robot-pc:~/catkin_ws/src$ catkin_init_workspace
Creating symlink "/home/robot/catkin_ws/src/CMakeLists.txt"
robot@robot-pc:~/catkin_ws/src$
robot@robot-pc:~/catkin_ws/src$
robot@robot-pc:~/catkin_ws/src$ ls
CMakeLists.txt
robot@robot-pc:~/catkin_ws/src$
```

***Figure 5-1.*** *The output of catkin_init_workspace*

There is a CMakeLists.txt inside the src folder.

After initializing the catkin workspace, you can build the workspace. You can able it to build the workspace without any packages. To build the workspace, switch from the catkin_ws/src folder to the catkin_ws folder.

```
$ ~/catkin_ws/src$ cd ..
```

The command to build the catkin workspace is catkin_make.

```
$ ~/catkin_ws$ catkin_make
```

You get the following output after entering this command (see Figure 5-2).

```
-- Using CATKIN_ENABLE_TESTING: ON
-- Call enable_testing()
-- Using CATKIN_TEST_RESULTS_DIR: /home/robot/catkin_ws/build/test_resu
-- Looking for pthread.h
-- Looking for pthread.h - found
-- Looking for pthread_create
-- Looking for pthread_create - not found
-- Looking for pthread_create in pthreads
-- Looking for pthread_create in pthreads - not found
-- Looking for pthread_create in pthread
-- Looking for pthread_create in pthread - found
-- Found Threads: TRUE
-- Found gtest sources under '/usr/src/gtest': gtests will be built
-- Using Python nosetests: /usr/bin/nosetests-2.7
-- catkin 0.7.6
-- BUILD_SHARED_LIBS is on
-- Configuring done
-- Generating done
-- Build files have been written to: /home/robot/catkin_ws/build
####
#### Running command: "make -j4 -l4" in "/home/robot/catkin_ws/build"
####
robot@robot-pc:~/catkin_ws$ ▓
```

***Figure 5-2.*** *The catkin_make output*

Now you can see a few folders in addition to the src folder
(see Figure 5-3).

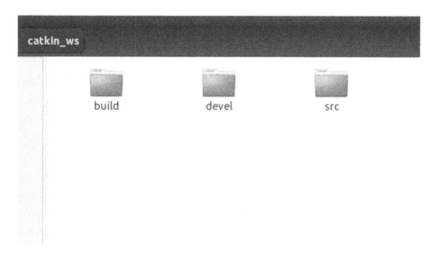

***Figure 5-3.*** *The catkin_ws folder after catkin_make command*

More information about the building process is in the next section.

The src folder is where our packages are kept. If you want to create or build a package, you have to copy those packages to the src folder.

After creating the workspace, it is important thing to add the workspace environment. This means you have to set the workspace path so that the packages inside the workspace become accessible and visible. To do this, you have to do the following steps.

Open the .bashrc file in the home folder and add the following line at the end of the file.

At a terminal, switch to the home folder and select the .bashrc file.

```
$ gedit .bashrc
```

Add the following line at the end of .bashrc (see Figure 5-4).

```
source ~/catkin_ws/devel/setup.bash
```

```
if ! shopt -oq posix; then
   if [ -f /usr/share/bash-completion/bash
      . /usr/share/bash-completion/bash_com
   elif [ -f /etc/bash_completion ]; then
      . /etc/bash_completion
   fi
fi
source /opt/ros/kinetic/setup.bash

source ~/catkin_ws/devel/setup.bash
```

*Figure 5-4.*  *Adding catkin_ws to .bashrc file*

As you already know, the `.bashrc` script in the home folder executes when a new terminal session starts. So, the command inserted in the `.bashrc` file also executes.

`setup.bash` in the following command has variables to add to the Linux environment.

```
source ~/catkin_ws/devel/setup.bash
```

When we source this file, the workspace path is added in the current terminal session. Now when we use any terminal, we can access the packages inside this workspace.

Before discussing the creation of packages, we need to discuss the catkin build system in ROS. You get a better idea about the building process when you are aware of the catkin build system.

## ROS Build System

Chapters 2 and 3 discussed the build system, which is nothing but tools to compile a set of source code and create target executables from it. The target can be an executable or a library. In ROS, there is a build system for compiling ROS packages. The name of the build system that we are using is *catkin* (`http://wiki.ros.org/catkin`). catkin is a custom build system made from the CMake build system and Python scripting. So why not directly use CMake? The answer is simple: building a set of ROS packages is complicated. The complexity increases with the number of packages and package dependencies. The catkin build system take cares of all these things.

You can read more about the catkin build system at `http://wiki.ros.org/catkin/conceptual_overview`.

# ROS Catkin Workspace

We have created a catkin workspace, but didn't discuss how it works. The workspace has several folders. Let's look at the function of each folder.

## src Folder

The src folder inside the catkin workspace folder is the place where you can create, or clone, new packages from repositories. ROS packages only build and create an executable when it is in the src folder. When we execute the catkin_make command from the workspace folder, it checks inside the src folder and build each packages.

## build Folder

When we run the catkin_make command from the ROS workspace, the catkin tool creates some build files and intermediate cache CMake files inside the build folder. These cache files help prevent from rebuilding all the packages when running the catkin_make command; for example, if you build five packages, and then add a new package to the src folder, only the new package builds during the next catkin_make command. This is because of those cache files inside the build folder. If you delete the build folder, all the packages build again.

## devel Folder

When we run the catkin_make command, each package is built, and if the build process is successful, the target executable is created. The executable is stored inside the devel folder, which has shell script files to add the current workspace to the ROS workspace path. We can access the current workspace packages only if we run this script. Generally, the following command is used to do this.

```
source ~/<workspace_name>/devel/setup.bash
```

We are adding this command in the `.bashrc` file, so that we can access the workspace packages in all terminal sessions. If you go through the procedures to set up the catkin workspace, you see these steps.

## install Folder

After building the target executable locally, run the following command to install the executable.

```
$ catkin_make install
```

It has to execute from the ROS workspace folder. If you do this, you see the `install` folder in the workspace. This folder keeps the install target files. When we run the executable, it executes from the `install` folder.

There is more information about the catkin workspace at `http://wiki.ros.org/catkin/workspaces#Catkin_Workspaces`.

# Creating a ROS Package

We are done creating the ROS workspace. Next, let's look at how to create a ROS package. The ROS package is where ROS nodes are organized— libraries and so forth. We can create a catkin ROS package by using the following command.

Synatx:

```
$ catkin_create_pkg ros_package_name package_dependencies
```

The command that we use to create the package is `catkin_create_pkg`. The first parameter for this command is the package name, and the dependencies of the package follow it; for example, we are going to create a package called `hello_world` with dependencies. We discuss more about the dependencies in the next section.

You have to execute the command from the `src` folder in the catkin workspace.

```
$ /catkin_ws/src$ catkin_create_pkg hello_world roscpp rospy
std_msgs
```

The output of this command is shown in Figure 5-5. This is how we create ROS packages.

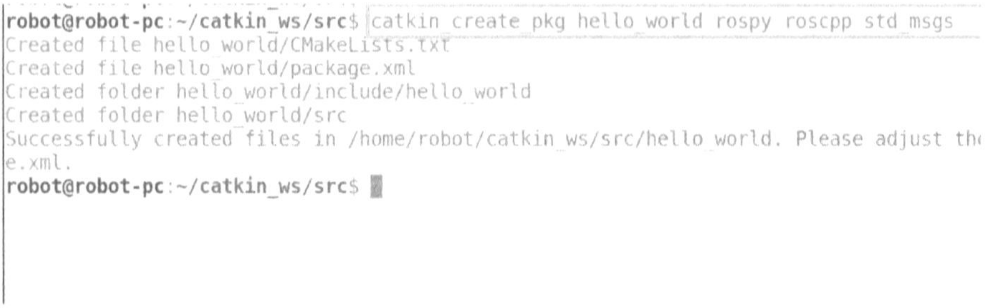

```
robot@robot-pc:~/catkin_ws/src$ catkin_create_pkg hello_world rospy roscpp std_msgs
Created file hello_world/CMakeLists.txt
Created file hello_world/package.xml
Created folder hello_world/include/hello_world
Created folder hello_world/src
Successfully created files in /home/robot/catkin_ws/src/hello_world. Please adjust the
e.xml.
robot@robot-pc:~/catkin_ws/src$ ▯
```

***Figure 5-5.*** *Output of catkin_create_pkg command*

The structure of a ROS package is shown in Figure 5-6.

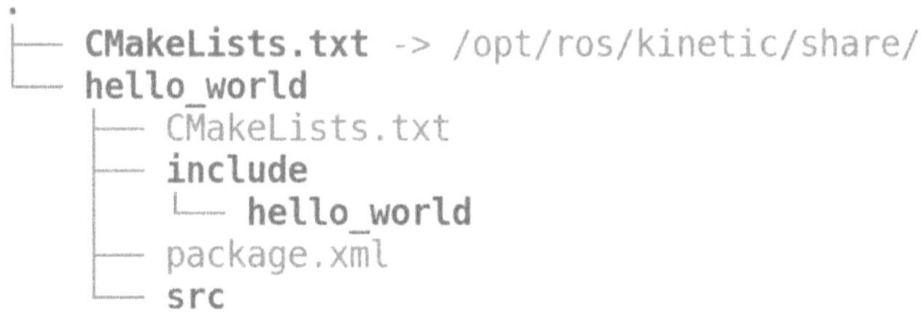

```
├── CMakeLists.txt -> /opt/ros/kinetic/share/
└── hello_world
    ├── CMakeLists.txt
    ├── include
    │   └── hello_world
    ├── package.xml
    └── src
```

***Figure 5-6.*** *Output of catkin_create_pkg command*

Inside the package is the src folder, package.xml, CMakeLists.txt, and the include folder.

- CMakeLists.txt: This file has all the commands to build the ROS source code inside the package and create the executable.

- `package.xml`: This is basically an XML file. It mainly contains the package dependencies, information, and so forth.

- `src`: The source code of ROS packages are kept in this folder. Normally, C++ files are kept in the `src` folder. If you want to keep Python scripts, you can create another folder called `scripts` inside the `package` folder.

- `include`: This folder contains the package header files. It can be automatically generated, or third-party library files go in it.

The next section discusses ROS client libraries, which are used to create ROS nodes.

# Using ROS Client Libraries

We have covered various ROS concepts like topics, services, messages, and so forth. How do we implement these concepts? The answer is by using ROS client libraries. The ROS client libraries are a collection of code with functions to implement ROS concepts. We can simply include these library functions in our code to make it a ROS node. The client library saves development time because it provides the built-in functions to make a ROS application.

We can write ROS nodes in any programming language. If there is any ROS client for that programming language, it is easier to create ROS nodes; otherwise, we may need to implement our own ROS concepts.

The following are the main ROS client libraries.

- *roscpp*: This is the ROS client library for C++. It is widely used for developing ROS applications because of its high performance.

- *rospy*: This is the ROS client library for Python (`http://wiki.ros.org/rospy`). Its advantage is saving development time. We can create a ROS node in less time than with roscpp. It is ideal for quick prototyping applications, but performance is weaker than with roscpp. Most of the command line tools in ROS are coded using rospy such as roslaunch, roscore and so forth.

- *roslisp*: This is the ROS client library of the Lisp language. It is mainly used in motion planning libraries on ROS, but it is not as popular as roscpp and rospy.

There are also experimental client libraries, including rosjava, rosnodejs, and roslua. The complete list of ROS client libraries is at `http://wiki.ros.org/Client%20Libraries`.

We will mainly work with roscpp and rospy. The next section shows a basic example of ROS nodes created using roscpp and rospy.

# roscpp and rospy

This section discusses the various aspects of writing a node using client libraries such as roscpp and rospy. This includes the header files and modules used in ROS nodes, initializing a ROS node, publishing and subscribing a topic, and so forth.

## Header Files and ROS Modules

When you write code in C++, the first section includes the header files. Similarly, when you write Python code, the first section imports Python modules. In this section, we look at the important headers files, and modules that we need to import into a ROS node.

To create a ROS C++ node, we have to include the following header files.

```
#include "ros/ros.h"
```

The ros.h has all the headers required to implement ROS functionalities. We can't create a ROS node without including this header file.

The next type of header file used in ROS nodes is a ROS message header. If we want to use a specific message type in our node, we have to include the message header file. ROS has some built-in message definition, and the user can also create a new message definition. There is a built-in message package in ROS called std_msgs that has a message definition of standard data types, such as int, float, string, and so forth. For example, if we want to include a string message in our code, we can use the following line of code.

```
#include "std_msgs/String.h"
```

Here, the first part is the package name and the next part is the message type name. If there is a custom message type, we can call it with the following syntax.

```
# include "msg_pkg_name/message_name.h"
```

The following are some of the messages in the std_msgs package.

```
# include "std_msgs/Int32.h"
# include "std_msgs/Int64.h"
```

The complete list of message types inside the std_msgs package is at http://wiki.ros.org/std_msgs.

In Python, we have to import modules to create a ROS node. The ROS module that we need to import is

```
import rospy
```

rospy has all the important ROS functions. To import a message type, we have to import the specific modules, like we did in C++.

The following is an example of importing a string message type in Python.

```
from std_msgs.msg import String
```

We have to use package_name.msg and import the required message type.

182

# Initializing a ROS Node

Before starting any ROS node, the first function called initializes the node. This is a mandatory step in any ROS node.

In C++, we initialize using the following line of code.

```
int main(int argc, char **argv)
{

ros::init(argc, argv, "name_of_node")
..................

}
```

After the int main() function, we have to include ros::init(), which initializes the ROS node. We can pass the argc,argv command-line arguments to the init() function and the name of the node. This is the ROS node name, and we can retrieve its list by using rosnode list.

In Python, we use the following line of code.

```
rospy.init_node('name_of_node', anonymous=True);
```

The first argument is the name of the node, and the second argument is anonymous=True, which means the node can run on multiple instances.

# Printing Messages in a ROS Node

ROS provides APIs to log messages. These messages are readable string that convey the status of the node.

In C++, the following functions log the node's messages.

```
ROS_INFO(string_msg,args): Logging the information of node
ROS_WARN(string_msg,args): Logging warning of the node
ROS_DEBUG(string_msg ,args): Logging debug messages
ROS_ERROR(string_msg ,args): Logging error messages
ROS_FATAL(string_msg ,args): Logging Fatal messages

Eg: ROS_DEBUG("Hello %s","World");
```

In Python, there are different functions for the logging operations.

```
rospy.logdebug(msg, *args)
rospy.logerr(msg, *args)
rospy.logfatal(msg, *args)
rospy.loginfo(msg, *args)
rospy.logwarn(msg, *args)
```

## Creating a Node Handle

After initializing the node, we have to create a NodeHandle instance that starts the ROS node and other operations, like publishing/subscribing a topic. We are using the ros::NodeHandle instance to create those operations.

In C++, the following shows how to create an instance of ros::NodeHandle.

```
ros::NodeHandle nh;
```

The rest of the operations in the node use the nh instance. In Python, we don't need to create a handle; the rospy module internally handles it.

## Creating a ROS Message Definition

Before publishing a topic, we have to create a ROS message definition. The message definition is created by using the following methods.

In C++, we can create an instance of a ROS message with the following line of code; for example, this is how we create an instance of std_msgs/ String.

```
std_msgs::String msg;
```

After creating the instance of the ROS message, we can add the data by using the following line of code.

```
msg.data = "String data"
```

In Python, we use the following line of code to add data to the string message.

```
msg = String()
msg.data = "string data"
```

## Publishing a Topic in ROS Node

This section shows how to publish a topic in a ROS node.

In C++, we use the following syntax.

```
ros::Publisher publisher_object = node_handle.advertise<ROS
message type >("topic_name",1000)
```

After creating the `publisher` object, the `publish()` command sends the ROS message through the topic.

```
publisher_object.publish(message)
```

Example:

```
ros::Publisher chatter_pub = nh.advertise<std_
msgs::String>("chatter", 1000);
```

```
chatter_pub.publish(msg);
```

In this example, `chatter_pub` is the ROS `publisher` instance, and it is going to publishing a topic with message type `std_msgs/String` and chatter as the topic name. The queue size is 1000.

In Python, the publishing syntax is as follows.

Syntax:

```
publisher_instance = rospy.Publisher('topic_name', message_
type, queue_size)
```

Example:

```
pub = rospy.Publisher('chatter', String, queue_size=10)
pub.publish(hello_str)
```

This example publishes a topic called chatter with a std_msgs/String message type and a queue_size of 10.

## Subscribing a Topic in ROS Node

When publishing a topic, we have to create a message type and need to send through the topic. When subscribing a topic, the message is received from the topic.

In C++, the following is the syntax of subscribing a topic.

```
ros::Subscriber subscriber_obj = nodehandle.subscribe
("topic_name", 1000, callback function)
```

When subscribing a topic, we don't need to mention the topic message type, but we do need to mention the topic name and a callback function. The callback function is a user-defined function that executes once a ROS message is received over the topic. Inside the callback, we can manipulate the ROS message—print it or make a decision based on the message data. (Callback is discussed in the next section.)

The following is a subscription example of the "chatter" topic with the "chatterCallback" callback function.

```
ros::Subscriber sub = n.subscribe("chatter", 1000,
chatterCallback);
```

The following shows how to subscribe a topic in Python.

```
rospy.Subscriber("topic_name",message_type,callback funtion name")
```

The following shows how to subscribe the "chatter" topic with the message type as string, and a callback function. In Python, we have to mention the message type along with the Subscriber() function.

```
rospy.Subscriber("chatter", String, callback)
```

## Writing the Callback Function in ROS Node

When we subscribe a ROS topic and a message arrives in that topic, the callback function is triggered. You may have seen the mention of a callback function in the subscriber function. The following is the syntax and an example of callback function in C++.

```
void callback_name(const ros_message_const_pointer &pointer)
{
// Access data
pointer->data

}
```

The following shows how to handle a ROS string message and print the data.

```
void chatterCallback(const std_msgs::String::ConstPtr& msg)
{
  ROS_INFO("I heard: [%s]", msg->data.c_str());
}
```

The following shows how to write a callback in Python. It's very similar to a Python function, which has an argument that holds the message data.

```
def callback(data):
    rospy.loginfo(rospy.get_caller_id() + "I heard %s", data.data)
```

# The ROS Spin Function in ROS Node

After starting the subscription or publishing, we may have to call a function to process the request to subscribe and publish. In a C++ node, the ros::spinOnce() function should be called after publishing a topic, and the ros::spin() function should be called if you are only subscribing a topic. If you are doing both, use the spinOnce() function.

In Python, there is no spin() function, but you can use the rospy. sleep() function after publishing, or the rospy.spin() function if there is only subscription of the topic.

# The ROS Sleep Function in ROS Node

If we want to make a constant rate inside a loop that is inside a node, we can use ros::Rate. We can create an instance of ros::Rate and mention the desired rate that we want. After creating the instance, we have to call the sleep() function inside it to get the rate in effect.

The following is an example of getting 10 Hz in C++.

```
ros::Rate r(10); // 10 hz

r.sleep();
```

The following is how to do it in Python.

```
rate = rospy.Rate(10) # 10hz

rate.sleep()
```

# Setting and Getting a ROS Parameter

In C++, we use the following line of code to access a parameter in our code. Basically, we have to declare a variable and use the getParam() function inside the node_handle to access the desired parameter.

```
std::string global_name;
```

```
if (nh.getParam("/global_name", global_name))
{
  ...
}
```

The following shows how to set a ROS parameter. The name and the value should be mentioned inside the setParam() function.

```
nh.setParam("/global_param", 5);
```

In Python, we can do the same thing using the following line of code.

```
global_name = rospy.get_param("/global_name")

rospy.set_param('~private_int', '2')
```

# The Hello World Example Using ROS

In this section, you are going to create a basic package called hello_world, and a publisher node and a subscriber node to send a "Hello World" string message. You also learn how to write a node in C++ and Python.

## Creating a hello_world Package

In ROS, the programs organized as packages. So we have to create a ROS package before writing any program.

To create a ROS package, we have to give a name of the package, then the dependent packages which help to compile the programs inside the package. For example, if your package has C++ program, you have to add 'roscpp' as dependency and if it is python, you have to add 'rospy' as dependency.

Before creating the package, first switch to the src folder.

```
$ catkin_ws/src$ catkin_create_pkg hello_world roscpp rospy
std_msgs
```

Figure 5-7 shows the output when we execute this command.

189

```
robot@robot-pc:~/catkin_ws/src$ catkin_create_pkg hello_world roscpp rospy std_msgs
Created file hello_world/CMakeLists.txt
Created file hello_world/package.xml
Created folder hello_world/include/hello_world
Created folder hello_world/src
Successfully created files in /home/robot/catkin_ws/src/hello_world. Please adjust t
robot@robot-pc:~/catkin_ws/src$ 
```

***Figure 5-7.***  *The output of catkin_create_pkg*

Now we can explore the different files created. The first important file is package.xml. As discussed, this file has information about the package and its dependencies.

The package.xml file definition is shown in Figure 5-8. Actually, when we create the package, it also has some commented code. All comments have been removed here to make it cleaner.

```xml
<?xml version="1.0"?>
<package>
  <name>hello_world</name>
  <version>0.0.0</version>
  <description>The hello_world package</description>
  <maintainer email="robot@todo.todo">robot</maintainer>
  <license>TODO</license>

  <buildtool_depend>catkin</buildtool_depend>
  <build_depend>roscpp</build_depend>
  <build_depend>rospy</build_depend>
  <build_depend>std_msgs</build_depend>
  <run_depend>roscpp</run_depend>
  <run_depend>rospy</run_depend>
  <run_depend>std_msgs</run_depend>

  <export>
  </export>

</package>
```

***Figure 5-8.***  *The package.xml definition*

190

You can edit this file and add dependencies, package information, and other information to the package. You can learn more about package.xml at http://wiki.ros.org/catkin/package.xml.

Figure 5-9 shows what the CMakeLists.txt file looks like.

```
cmake_minimum_required(VERSION 2.8.3)
project(hello_world)


find_package(catkin REQUIRED COMPONENTS
  roscpp
  rospy
  std_msgs
)


catkin_package()

include_directories(
  ${catkin_INCLUDE_DIRS}
)
```

***Figure 5-9.*** *The CMakeLists.txt definition*

In this file, the minimum version of CMake required to build the package and the project name is at the top of the file.

The find_package() finds the necessary dependencies of this package. If these packages are not available, we can't able to build this package. The catkin_package() is a catkin-provide CMake macro used for specifying catkin-specific information to the build system.

You can learn more about CMakeLists.txt at http://wiki.ros.org/catkin/CMakeLists.txt.

A good reference for creating a ROS package is at http://wiki.ros.org/ROS/Tutorials/catkin/CreatingPackage.

## Creating a ROS C++ Node

After creating the package, the next step is to create the ROS nodes. The C++ code is kept in the src folder.

The following is the first ROS node. It's a C++ node to publish a "Hello World" string message. You can save it under src/talker.cpp.

```
#include "ros/ros.h"
#include "std_msgs/String.h"
#include <sstream>

int main(int argc, char **argv)
{
  ros::init(argc, argv, "talker");

  ros::NodeHandle n;

  ros::Publisher chatter_pub = n.advertise<std_
  msgs::String>("chatter", 1000);

  ros::Rate loop_rate(10);

  int count = 0;

  while (ros::ok())
  {
    std_msgs::String msg;

    std::stringstream ss;

    ss << "hello world " << count;

    msg.data = ss.str();

    ROS_INFO("%s", msg.data.c_str());

    chatter_pub.publish(msg);

    ros::spinOnce();
```

```
    loop_rate.sleep();

    ++count;
  }

  return 0;
}
```

The code is self-explanatory. Basically, it creates a new string message instance and a publisher instance. After creating both, it adds data to the string message along with a count. After adding the data, it publishes the topic, "/chatter. You can also see the usage of the ros::spinOnce() function here. The code executes until you press Ctrl+C.

Next, you see the listener.cpp, which subscribes the topic published by talker.cpp. After getting data from the topic, it prints that message.

```
#include "ros/ros.h"
#include "std_msgs/String.h"

void chatterCallback(const std_msgs::String::ConstPtr& msg)
{

  ROS_INFO("I heard: [%s]", msg->data.c_str());

}

int main(int argc, char **argv)
{

  ros::init(argc, argv, "listener");

  ros::NodeHandle n;

  ros::Subscriber sub = n.subscribe("chatter", 1000, chatterCallback);

  ros::spin();

  return 0;
}
```

In `listener.cpp`, the "chatter" topic is subscribing and registering a callback function for the topic, which is `chatterCallback`. The callback is defined at the beginning of the code. Whenever a message comes to the "chatter" topic, this callback is executed. Inside the callback, the data in the message is printed.

`ros::spin()` executes the subscribe callbacks and helps the node remain in a wait state, so it won't quit until you press Ctrl+C.

## Editing the CMakeLists.txt File

After saving the two files in the `hello_world/src` folder, the nodes need to be compiled to create the executable. To do this, we have to edit the `CMakeLists.txt` file, which is not too complicated. We need to add four lines of code to `CMakeLists.txt`. Figure 5-10 shows the additional lines of code to insert.

```
include_directories(
  ${catkin_INCLUDE_DIRS}
)

add_executable(talker src/talker.cpp)
 target_link_libraries(talker
   ${catkin_LIBRARIES}
 )

add_executable(listener src/listener.cpp)
 target_link_libraries(listener
   ${catkin_LIBRARIES}
 )
```

***Figure 5-10.*** *Adding building instructions inside CMakeLists.txt*

You can see that we are adding add_executable() and target_
link_libraries() to CMakeLists.txt. add_executable() creates the
executable from the source code. The first parameter is the executable
name, which links with the libraries. If these two processes are successful,
we get executable nodes.

## Building C++ Nodes

After saving CMakeLists.txt, we can build the source code. The command
to build the nodes is catkin_make. Just switch to the workspace folder and
execute the catkin_make command.

To switch to the catkin_ws folder, assume that the workspace is in the
home folder.

```
$ cd ~/catkin_ws
```

Executing the catkin_make command to build the nodes
```
$ catkin_make
```

If everything is correct, you get a message saying that the build was
successful (see Figure 5-11).

```
Scanning dependencies of target listener
Scanning dependencies of target talker
[ 25%] Building CXX object hello_world/CMakeFiles/listener.dir/src/listener.cpp.o
[ 50%] Building CXX object hello_world/CMakeFiles/talker.dir/src/talker.cpp.o
[ 75%] Linking CXX executable /home/robot/catkin_ws/devel/lib/hello_world/talker
[100%] Linking CXX executable /home/robot/catkin_ws/devel/lib/hello_world/listener
[100%] Built target listener
[100%] Built target talker
robot@robot-pc:~/catkin_ws$
```

***Figure 5-11.*** *Building messages in the terminal*

So we have successfully built the nodes. Now what? We can execute
these nodes, right? That is covered in the next section.

# Executing C++ Nodes

After building the nodes, the executables are generated inside the catkin_
ws/devel/lib/hello_world/ folder (see Figure 5-12).

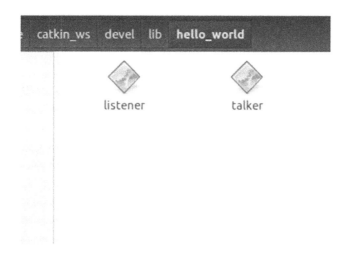

catkin_ws | devel | lib | **hello_world**

listener                 talker

***Figure 5-12.***  *Generated executable*

After creating the executable, we can run it on a Linux terminal.
Open three terminals, and execute each command one by one.

Starting roscore

$ roscore

The following command starts the talker node. We can use the rosrun
command to start the node.

$ rosrun hello_world talker

The node prints messages on the terminal. Check the list of ROS topics
in the system by using the following command.

$ rostopic list

You see the following topics.

```
/chatter
/rosout
/rosout_agg
```

'chatter is the topic published by the talker node. The /rosout topics are for logging purposes. It start publishing when we execute the roscore command.

The listener node can start in another terminal.

```
$ rosrun hello_world listener
```

Figure 5-13 shows the message data from the /chatter topic.

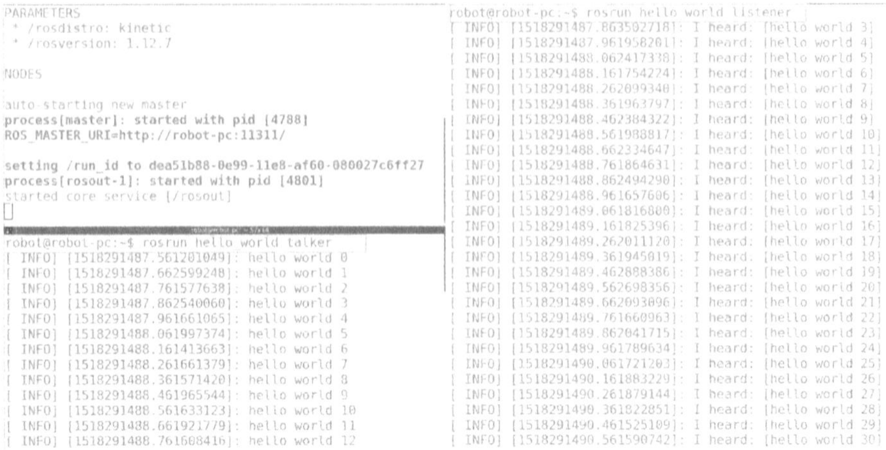

***Figure 5-13.***  *Output of talker and listener C++ nodes*

You can close each terminal by pressing the Ctrl+C key combination. Next, we look at the talker and listener nodes in Python.

## Creating Python Nodes

We can make a folder called script inside the package, and we can keep the Python scripts inside this folder (scripts/talker.py). The first program that we are going to discuss is talker.py.

```python
import rospy
from std_msgs.msg import String

def talker():

    rospy.init_node('talker', anonymous=True)
    pub = rospy.Publisher('chatter', String, queue_size=10)
    rate = rospy.Rate(10) # 10hz

    while not rospy.is_shutdown():
        hello_str = "hello world %s" % rospy.get_time()
        rospy.loginfo(hello_str)
        pub.publish(hello_str)
        rate.sleep()

if __name__ == '__main__':
    try:
        talker()
    except rospy.ROSInterruptException:
        pass
```

In the talker.py code, in the beginning, we can see, we are importing the rospy module and ros message modules. In the talker() function, we can see the initialization of ROS node, the creation of a new ROS publisher. After initializing the node, we are using a while loop to publish a string message called "Hello World" to the /chatter topic. The working of this node is same as talker.cpp that we already discussed.

The subscribing node, called listener.py, should be kept inside scripts/listener.py.

```python
import rospy
from std_msgs.msg import String

def callback(data):
    rospy.loginfo(rospy.get_caller_id() + "I heard %s", data.data)

def listener():

    # In ROS, nodes are uniquely named. If two nodes with the same
    # node are launched, the previous one is kicked off. The
    # anonymous=True flag means that rospy will choose a unique
    # name for our 'talker' node so that multiple talkers can
    # run simultaneously.
    rospy.init_node('listener', anonymous=True)

    rospy.Subscriber("chatter", String, callback)

    # spin() simply keeps python from exiting until this node
      is stopped
    rospy.spin()

if __name__ == '__main__':
    listener()
```

The node is similar to listener.cpp. We are initializing the node and creating a subscriber on the /chatter topic. After subscribing the topic, it waits for ROS messages. The waiting is done with the rospy.spin() function. Inside the callback() function, the message is printed.

# Executing Python Nodes

In this section, we see how to execute the nodes. There is no need to compile the Python nodes. We can just execute it using the following commands. You can see the output of the commands from Figure 5-14.

Start the roscore

```
$ roscore
```

Start the talker.py

```
$ rosrun hello_world talker.py
```

Start the listener.py

```
$ rosrun hello_world listener.py
```

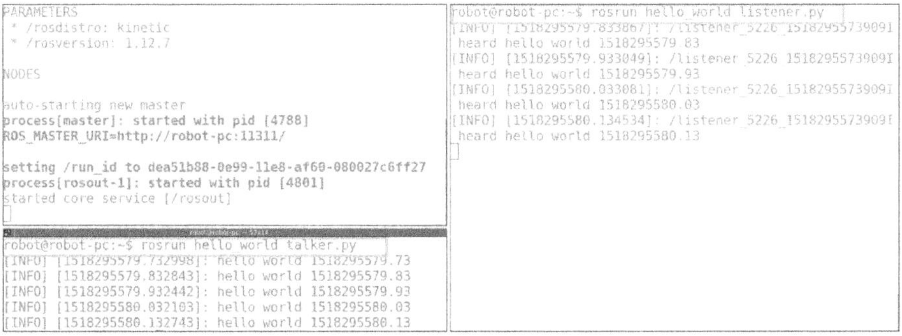

***Figure 5-14.***   *Output of talker and listener Python nodes*

# Creating Launch Files

This section discusses how to write launch files for C++ and Python nodes. The advantage of ROS launch files is that we can run any number of nodes in a single command.

We can create a folder called launch inside the package and keep the launch files in that folder.

The following is `talker_listener.launch`, which can run C++ executables.

```
<launch>
  <node name="listener_node" pkg="hello_world" type="listener"
  output="screen"/>
  <node name="talker_node" pkg="hello_world" type="talker"
  output="screen"/>
</launch>
```

This launch file can run the talker and listener nodes in one shot. The package name of the node is in the pkg= field and the name of the executable is in the type= field. You can assign any name to the node. It is better if it is similar to the executable name.

After saving the launch file inside the launch folder, you may have to change the permission of the executable.

The following shows how to do that.

```
$ hello_world/launch$ sudo chmod +x talker_listener.launch
```

The following is the command to execute this launch file. We can execute it from any terminal path.

```
$ roslaunch hello_world talker_listener.launch
```

After the `roslaunch` command, use the package name and then the launch file name.

Figure 5-15 shows the output.

```
 listener_node (hello_world/listener)
 talker_node (hello_world/talker)

auto-starting new master
process[master]: started with pid [5635]
ROS_MASTER_URI=http://localhost:11311

setting /run_id to 1736ac68-0ea5-11e8-af60-080027c6ff27
process[rosout-1]: started with pid [5648]
started core service [/rosout]
process[listener_node-2]: started with pid [5656]
process[talker_node-3]: started with pid [5670]
[ INFO] [1518296286.432156336]: hello world 0
[ INFO] [1518296286.532936503]: hello world 1
[ INFO] [1518296286.632730963]: hello world 2
[ INFO] [1518296286.733540586]: hello world 3
[ INFO] [1518296286.733994769]: I heard: [hello world 3]
[ INFO] [1518296286.833653567]: hello world 4
[ INFO] [1518296286.834120072]: I heard: [hello world 4]
[ INFO] [1518296286.932997644]: hello world 5
[ INFO] [1518296286.933576537]: I heard: [hello world 5]
[ INFO] [1518296287.032813044]: hello world 6
[ INFO] [1518296287.033458823]: I heard: [hello world 6]
[ INFO] [1518296287.133145129]: hello world 7
```

***Figure 5-15.*** *Output of talker_listener.launch file*

To launch the Python nodes, use the following launch file. You can save it as launch/talker_listener_python.launch.

```
<launch>
  <node name="listener_node" pkg="hello_world" type="listener.py"
  output="screen"/>

  <node name="talker_node" pkg="hello_world" type="talker.py"
  output="screen"/>
</launch>
```

After saving it, change the permissions of the file too.

```
$ hello_world/launch$ sudo chmod +x talker_listener_python.launch
```

Then execute the launch file using the roslaunch command.

```
$ roslaunch hello_world talker_listener_python.launch
```

The output is the same as with the C++ nodes. We can stop the launch file by pressing Ctrl+C in the terminal in which the launch file is running.

## Visualizing a Computing Graph

Do you want to see what's happening when the launch files are executing? The rqt_graph GUI tool visualizes the ROS computation graph.

Use any of the launch files that we created in the previous section.

```
$ roslaunch hello_world talker_listener.launch
```

And in another terminal, run the following.

```
$ rqt_graph
```

Figure 5-16 shows the output of this GUI tool.

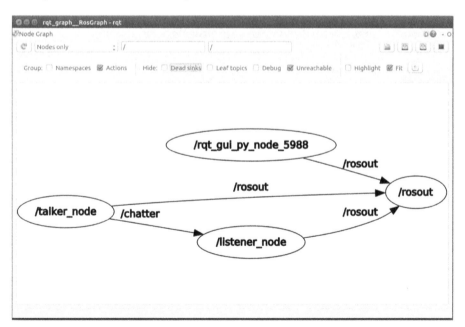

***Figure 5-16.*** *Output of rqt_graph tool*

In the graph, you see `talker_node`, which is the name given to `talker` in the launch file. `listener_node` is the name of the `listener` node. `/chatter` is the topic published by the `talker_node`. It is subscribed by the `listener_node`.

All the debug messages from these two nodes are going to `/rosout`. The debug messages are message that we printed using ROS debug functions (`http://wiki.ros.org/roscpp/Over view/Logging`). We have already discussed those functions. The `/rqt_gui` node is also sending debug statements to `/rosout`.

This is how the ROS computation graph works.

# Programming turtlesim Using rospy

We are done with the "Hello World" ROS example in C++ and Python. In this section, we use a more interesting application. We saw the turtlesim application in ROS. Now we look at how to program turtlesim using rospy Py. We are using rospy for the demo because it is very simple to prototype. In turtlesim, there is a turtle that we can move around the workspace.

## Moving turtlesim

This section discusses how to program turtlesim to move around its workspace.

You already know how to start the turtlesim application. The following is the list of commands to run.

Starting roscore

```
$ roscore
```

Running turtlesim node in another terminal

```
$ rosrun turtlesim turtlesim_node
```

Here is the list of topics which is publishing by turtlesim_node

```
$ rostopic list
```

```
/rosout
/rosout_agg
/turtle1/cmd_vel
/turtle1/color_sensor
/turtle1/pose
```

To move the turtle inside the turtlesim application, publish the linear and angular velocity to the /turtle1/cmd_vel topic.

Check the type of the /turtle1/cmd_vel topic by using the following command.

```
$ rostopic type /turtle1/cmd_vel
```

```
geometry_msgs/Twist
```

This means that the /cmd_vel topic has the geometry_msgs/Twist message type, so we have to publish the same message type to this topic to move the robot.

To see the geometry_msgs/Twist definition, use the following command.

```
$ rosmsg show geometry_msgs/Twist
```

The output of the command is shown in Figure 5-17.

```
robot@robot-pc:~$ rosmsg show geometry_msgs/Twist
geometry_msgs/Vector3 linear
  float64 x
  float64 y
  float64 z
geometry_msgs/Vector3 angular
  float64 x
  float64 y
  float64 z
```

***Figure 5-17.*** *Definition of geometry_msgs/Twist message*

The twist message has two subsections: linear velocity and angular velocity.

If we set the robot's linear velocity component, it moves forward or backward. In turtlesim, we can only set the linear.x component because it can move only in x direction; there is no motion along y and z. Also, we can set angular.z components to rotate the robot on its axis. There is no effect to other components.

More information about this message is at `http://docs.ros.org/api/geometry_msgs/html/msg/Twist.html`.

How can we move the topic through the command line? By using rostopic. The following command publishes the linear.x = 0.1 velocity to the turtlesim node.

---

**Note**   You don't need to enter the complete command. Use the Tab key to autocomplete the command. Just type **rostopic pub /turtle1/cmd_vel**, and use the Tab key to autocomplete other fields.

---

```
$ rostopic pub /turtle1/cmd_vel geometry_msgs/Twist "linear:
        x:0.1
        y:0
        z:0
angular:
        x:0
        y:0
        z:0"
```

How do we move the turtle in a Python node?

We are going to create a new node called move_turtle and publish a twist message to the turtlesim node. Figure 5-18 shows the communication between the two nodes.

**Figure 5-18.** *Computation graph of move_turtle node and turtlesim node*

The following is the code for the move_turtle.py node. You can read the comments in the code to get a better idea about each line of code.

```
#!/usr/bin/env python

import rospy

#Importing Twist message: Used to send velocity to Turtlesim
from geometry_msgs.msg import Twist

#Handling command line arguments
import sys

#Function to move turtle: Linear and angular velocities are
arguments
def move_turtle(lin_vel,ang_vel):

    rospy.init_node('move_turtle', anonymous=False)

        #The /turtle1/cmd_vel is the topic in which we have to
        send Twist messages
    pub = rospy.Publisher('/turtle1/cmd_vel', Twist, queue_size=10)
    rate = rospy.Rate(10) # 10hz

        #Creating Twist message instance
    vel = Twist()

    while not rospy.is_shutdown():
```

```
        #Adding linear and angular velocity to the message
        vel.linear.x = lin_vel
        vel.linear.y = 0
        vel.linear.z = 0

        vel.angular.x = 0
        vel.angular.y = 0
        vel.angular.z = ang_vel

        rospy.loginfo("Linear Vel = %f: Angular Vel =
        %f",lin_vel,ang_vel)

        #Publishing Twist message
        pub.publish(vel)

        rate.sleep()

if __name__ == '__main__':
    try:
        #Providing linear and angular velocity through command line
        move_turtle(float(sys.argv[1]),float(sys.argv[2]))
    except rospy.ROSInterruptException:
        pass
```

This code takes the linear and the angular velocity through a command line. We can use the Python sys module to get the command-line arguments inside our code. Once it has the linear velocity and the angular velocity, it calls the move_turtle() function, which inserts both velocities into a twist message and publishes it.

You can save the code as move_turtle.py, and change the permission to executable.

The following shows how to run it.

```
Start roscore
```

```
$ roscore
```

Start the turtlesim node

```
$ rosrun turtlesim turtlesim_node
```

Run the move_turtle.py node along with the command-line arguments, which are 0.2 and 0.1. That is, linear velocity = 0.2 m/s and angular velocity = 0.1 rad/s.

```
$ rosrun hello_world move_turtle.py 0.2 0.1
```

You get the output shown in Figure 5-19 if you run this code. It creates a circle.

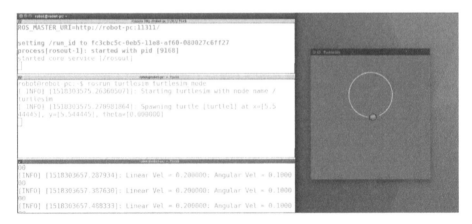

***Figure 5-19.*** *Output of move_turtle.py*

## Printing the Robot's Position

You have seen how to publish the turtle's velocity. Now you are going to learn how to get the turtle's current position from the /turtle1/pose topic.

Restart turtlesim_node and close move_turtle.py. Echo the /turtle1/pose topic using rostopic. The turtle's current position is shown in Figure 5-20.

```
$ rostopic echo /turtle1/pose
```

```
robot@robot-pc:~$ rostopic echo /turtle1/pose
x: 5.544444561
y: 5.544444561
theta: 0.0
linear_velocity: 0.0
angular_velocity: 0.0
- - -
x: 5.544444561
y: 5.544444561
theta: 0.0
linear_velocity: 0.0
angular_velocity: 0.0
- - -
x: 5.544444561
y: 5.544444561
theta: 0.0
linear_velocity: 0.0
angular_velocity: 0.0
- - -
```

***Figure 5-20.***  *Turtle pose from topic /turtle1/pose*

You see the current (x,y,theta) value of the robot and the turtle's current linear and angular velocities.

If you want to get this position in a Python node, you have to subscribe the called /turtle1/pose topic. To do that and get the data from the message, you have to know the ROS message type. The following finds the message type.

```
$ rostopic type /turtle1/pose
```

```
turtlsim/Pose
```

If you want to know the message definition, use the following command.

```
$ rosmsg show turtlesim/Pose
```

As shown in Figure 5-21, there are five terms inside the message: x, y, theta, linear velocity, and angular velocity.

```
robot@robot-pc:~$ rosmsg show turtlesim/Pose
float32 x
float32 y
float32 theta
float32 linear_velocity
float32 angular_velocity
```

***Figure 5-21.*** *ROS message definition of turtlesim/Pose*

To learn more about this message, refer to `http://docs.ros.org/api/turtlesim/html/msg/Pose.html`.

Let's modify the existing move_turtle.py and add the option to subscribe the /turtle1/pose topic. Save this code as move_turtle_get_pose.py.

Figure 5-22 shows how the program works. It is feeding velocity and subscribing the position from the turtlesim node at the same time.

***Figure 5-22.*** *move_turtle_get_pose.py code*

```
#!/usr/bin/env python

import rospy

from geometry_msgs.msg import Twist

from turtlesim.msg import Pose

import sys

#/turtle1/Pose topic callback
def pose_callback(pose):
        rospy.loginfo("Robot X = %f : Y=%f :
        Z=%f\n",pose.x,pose.y,pose.theta)

def move_turtle(lin_vel,ang_vel):
```

```
    rospy.init_node('move_turtle', anonymous=True)
    pub = rospy.Publisher('/turtle1/cmd_vel', Twist, queue_size=10)

        #Creating new subscriber: Topic name= /turtle1/pose:
        Callback name: pose_callback
    rospy.Subscriber('/turtle1/pose',Pose, pose_callback)

    rate = rospy.Rate(10) # 10hz

    vel = Twist()
    while not rospy.is_shutdown():

        vel.linear.x = lin_vel
        vel.linear.y = 0
        vel.linear.z = 0

        vel.angular.x = 0
        vel.angular.y = 0
        vel.angular.z = ang_vel

        rospy.loginfo("Linear Vel = %f: Angular Vel = %f",lin_
        vel,ang_vel)

        pub.publish(vel)

        rate.sleep()
if __name__ == '__main__':
    try:
        move_turtle(float(sys.argv[1]),float(sys.argv[2]))
    except rospy.ROSInterruptException:
        pass
```

This code is self-explanatory. You can see comments where the code for subscribing the /turtle1/pose topic is added.

Run the code by using the following commands. Figure 5-23 shows that the code is printing the robot's positon and velocity.

Starting roscore

$ roscore

Restarting the turtlesim node

$ rosrun turtlesim turtlesim_node

Running move_turtle_get_pose.py code

$ rosrun hello_world move_turtle_get_pose.py 0.2 0.1

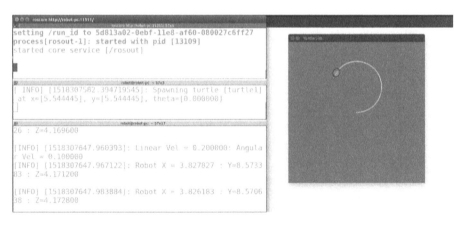

***Figure 5-23.*** *Output of move_turtle_get_pose.py code*

If we are getting both position and velocity, we can simply command the robot to move to a specific distance, right? The next example is moving the robot with distance feedback.

The code is a modification of the move_turtle_get_pose.py code.

## Moving the Robot with Position Feedback

We can save this code as move_distance.py. The communication between this node and turtlesim is shown in Figure 5-24.

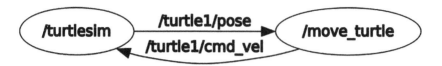

**Figure 5-24.** *Communication of move_distance.py to turtlesim*

This node is simple. We can give linear velocity, angular velocity, and distance (global distance) to it as a command-line argument.

Along with publishing velocity to the turtle, it checks the distance moved. When it reaches its destination, the turtle or robot stops. You can read the comments inside the code to understand what's happening inside the code.

```python
#!/usr/bin/env python

import rospy

from geometry_msgs.msg import Twist

from turtlesim.msg import Pose

import sys

robot_x = 0

def pose_callback(pose):
        global robot_x

        rospy.loginfo("Robot X = %f\n",pose.x)

        robot_x = pose.x

def move_turtle(lin_vel,ang_vel,distance):

    global robot_x

    rospy.init_node('move_turtle', anonymous=True)
    pub = rospy.Publisher('/turtle1/cmd_vel', Twist, queue_size=10)
```

```
rospy.Subscriber('/turtle1/pose',Pose, pose_callback)

rate = rospy.Rate(10) # 10hz

vel = Twist()
while not rospy.is_shutdown():

    vel.linear.x = lin_vel
    vel.linear.y = 0
    vel.linear.z = 0

    vel.angular.x = 0
    vel.angular.y = 0
    vel.angular.z = ang_vel

    #rospy.loginfo("Linear Vel = %f: Angular Vel = %f",
    lin_vel,ang_vel)

    #Checking the robot distance is greater than the
    commanded distance
    # If it is greater, stop the node

    if(robot_x >= distance):
            rospy.loginfo("Robot Reached destination")
            rospy.logwarn("Stopping robot")

            break

    pub.publish(vel)

    rate.sleep()
if __name__ == '__main__':
    try:
        move_turtle(float(sys.argv[1]),float(sys.argv[2]),
        float(sys.argv[3]))
    except rospy.ROSInterruptException:
        pass
```

We can run the code by using the following commands. You can Figure 5-25 for seeing the output

Start roscore

```
$ roscore
```

Start turtlesim node

```
$ rosrun turtlesim turtlesim_node
```

Run the move_distance.py. Mention linear, angular velocity and the global distance the robot should travel.

```
$ rosrun hello_world move_distance.py 0.2 0.0 8.0
```

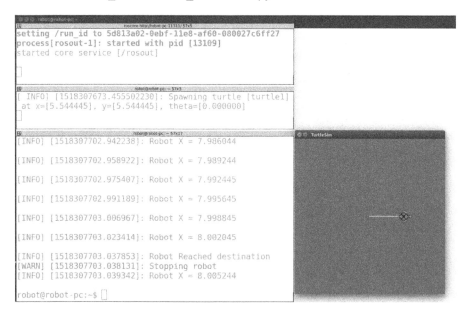

***Figure 5-25.*** *Output of move_distance.py*

We have played with lot of things in turtlesim using ROS topic. Now, we can work with ROS service and a ROS parameter. The next example simply resets the turtlesim workspace, and randomly changes the background color. The workspace reset is accomplished using ROS services, and the color changing is done using ROS parameter. When the workspace resets, the robot's position resets to the home position and the turtle model changes.

## Reset and Change the Background Color

This code shows how to call a service and a parameter from a Python code.

The following gets the list of services in the turtlesim node (see Figure 5-26).

```
$ rosservice list
```

```
robot@robot-pc:~$ rosservice list
/clear
/kill
/reset
/rosout/get_loggers
/rosout/set_logger_level
/spawn
/turtle1/set_pen
/turtle1/teleport_absolute
/turtle1/teleport_relative
/turtlesim/get_loggers
/turtlesim/set_logger_level
```

*Figure 5-26.* *List of turtlesim node services*

There are several services, but we want the /reset service. When we call this service, the workspace resets.

We can retrieve the type of service from the following topic.

```
$ rosservice type /reset
```

```
std_srvs/Empty
```

`std_srvs/Empty` is a built-in service from ROS. It has no fields.

The following command shows the field of the corresponding topic.

```
$ rossrv show std_srvs/Empty
```

---

We can also list the ROS parameters. You can see the turtlesim background color in three parameters. If we change these parameters, we change the color. After setting the color, we have to reset the workspace to show the new color (see Figure 5-27).

```
$ rosparam list
```

```
robot@robot-pc:~$ rosparam list
/background_b
/background_g
/background_r
/rosdistro
/roslaunch/uris/host_robot_pc__44371
/rosversion
/run_id
```

***Figure 5-27.***  *List of parameters from turtlesim node*

The following gets the value from each parameter.

```
$ rosparam get /background_b
```

255

```
robot@robot-pc:~$ rostopic echo /turtle1/color_sensor
r: 69
g: 86
b: 255
---
r: 69
g: 86
b: 255
---
r: 69
g: 86
b: 255
---
r: 69
g: 86
b: 255
---
```

***Figure 5-28.*** *Topic publishing the color*

The following topic publishes the background color (see Figure 5-28).

```
$ rostopic echo /turtle1/color_sensor
```

The following code sets the parameter for the background color and resets the workspace by calling /reset service.

```
#!/usr/bin/env python

import rospy

import random

from std_srvs.srv import Empty

def change_color():

    rospy.init_node('change_color', anonymous=True)

    #Setting random values from 0-255 in the color parameters
    rospy.set_param('/background_b',random.randint(0,255))
    rospy.set_param('/background_g',random.randint(0,255))
    rospy.set_param('/background_r',random.randint(0,255))
```

219

```
#Waiting for service /reset
rospy.wait_for_service('/reset')

#Calling /reset service
    try:

        serv = rospy.ServiceProxy('/reset',Empty)
        resp = serv()
        rospy.loginfo("Executed service")

    except rospy.ServiceException, e:
        rospy.loginfo("Service call failed: %s" %e)

    rospy.spin()

if __name__ == '__main__':
    try:
        change_color()
    except rospy.ROSInterruptException:
        pass
```

We can save the code as turtle_service_param.py. The following commands starts the ROS node (see Figure 5-29).

```
Starting roscore

$ roscore

Starting turtlesim_node

$ rosrun turtlesim turtlesim_node

Execute the turtle_service_param.py code

$ rosrun hello_world turtle_service_param.py
```

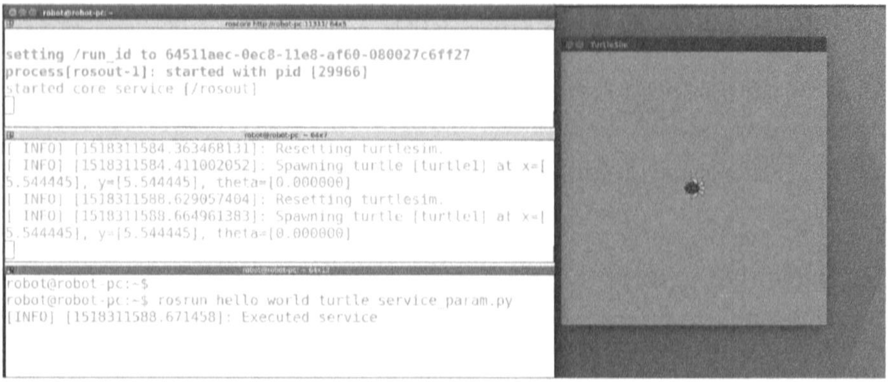

***Figure 5-29.*** *Resetting workspace and changing colors*

You have successfully done the turtlesim exercise. The turtle is actually a robot. You can do all of the operations that you did with the turtle with a physical robot too. The next section explains how to do this operation with an actual robot. It is only a simulation but uses the same procedure as with real hardware.

# Programming TurtleBot Simulation Using rospy

There are several robots available on the market that run completely on ROS and Ubuntu. The TurtleBot series are a low-cost robots that are used for education and research. You can learn more about the TurtleBot 2 robot at www.turtlebot.com/turtlebot2/. If you want to check out the latest version of a TurtleBot, go to http://emanual.robotis.com/docs/en/platform/turtlebot3/overview/.

In this section, we program TurtleBot 2. We look at the installation of TurtleBot 2 packages and how to start the simulation in Gazebo. The code that we developed for turtlesim works on the TurtleBot 2 and 3 robots. The first step is to install the TurtleBot 2 packages.

# Installing TurtleBot 2 Packages

The TurtleBot packages are already available in the ROS repository, so we just need to install them.

The first step is to update the list of packages by using the following command.

```
$ sudo apt-get update
```

Installing turtlebot simulation packages

```
$ sudo apt-get install ros-kinetic-turtlebot-gazebo ros-kinetic-turtlebot-simulator ros-kinetic-turtlebot-description ros-kinetic-turtlebot-teleop
```

These packages install the TurtleBot simulation environment in Ubuntu 16.04 LTS.

# Launching the TurtleBot Simulation

After installing the TurtleBot packages, launch the simulation of TurtleBot 2 by using the following command.

---

**Note**   It may take time to load the environment in Gazebo. Initially, the Gazebo window may be black because some 3D mesh files are downloading. The time it takes to complete the download depends on your Internet speed. If you feel that Gazebo is stuck, just cancel by pressing Ctrl+C, and launch it again.

---

```
$ roslaunch turtlebot_gazebo turtlebot_world.launch
```

This command launches a ROS launch file from the turtlebot_gazebo package. If the simulation loads successfully, you get a window like the one shown in Figure 5-30.

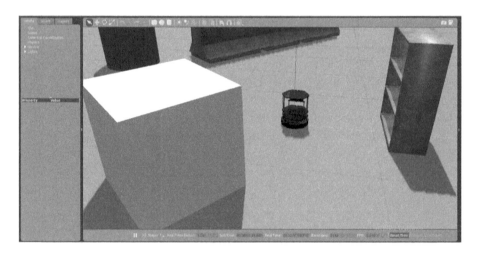

**Figure 5-30.** *TurtleBot 2 Gazebo simulation*

If you want to move the robot around the environment, start a new terminal and launch the following command.

```
$ roslaunch turtlebot_teleop keyboard_teleop.launch
```

When you run this command, you get the following messages on the terminal. Click the terminal using a mouse, and press the keys mentioned on the terminal. You can move the robot using I, J, and L keys (see Figure 5-31).

```
Control Your Turtlebot!
- - - - - - - - - - - - - - - - - - - - - - - - - - -
Moving around:
   u    i    o
   j    k    l
   m    ,    .

q/z : increase/decrease max speeds by 10%
w/x : increase/decrease only linear speed by 10%
e/c : increase/decrease only angular speed by 10%
space key, k : force stop
anything else : stop smoothly

CTRL-C to quit

currently:      speed 0.2       turn 1
```

**Figure 5-31.** *TurtleBot 2 teleop application*

If you want to stop the robot, press Space bar, if you want to stop the simulation or teleoperation, just press Ctrl+C.

## Moving a Fixed Distance Using a Python Node

In this section, we move the robot to a fixed distance using the node that we used for turtlesim. We can modify the move_distance.py node.

For turtlebot the velocity Twist message topic is: /cmd_vel_mux/input/teleop: Message type: geometry_msgs/Twist

Robot position feedback topic: /odom : Message type: nav_msgs/Odometry

We get the definition of odometry from the following command.

```
$ rosmsg show nav_msgs/Odometry
```

It is a built-in message type in ROS.

We have to import the modules for these messages. The logic of the robot movement is the same as in turtlesim. The distance is global distance. The initial origin of the robot is 0,0,0.

```
#!/usr/bin/env python

import rospy

from geometry_msgs.msg import Twist

from nav_msgs.msg import Odometry

import sys

robot_x = 0

def pose_callback(msg):
        global robot_x

        #Reading x position from the Odometry message
        robot_x = msg.pose.pose.position.x
```

```python
        rospy.loginfo("Robot X = %f\n",robot_x)

def move_turtle(lin_vel,ang_vel,distance):

    global robot_x

    rospy.init_node('move_turtlebot', anonymous=False)

    #The Twist topic is /cmd_vel_muc/input/teleop
    pub = rospy.Publisher('/cmd_vel_mux/input/teleop', Twist,
    queue_size=10)

    #Position topic is /odom
    rospy.Subscriber('/odom',Odometry, pose_callback)

    rate = rospy.Rate(10) # 10hz

    vel = Twist()
    while not rospy.is_shutdown():

        vel.linear.x = lin_vel
        vel.linear.y = 0
        vel.linear.z = 0

        vel.angular.x = 0
        vel.angular.y = 0
        vel.angular.z = ang_vel

        #rospy.loginfo("Linear Vel = %f: Angular Vel = %f",lin_
        vel,ang_vel)

        if(robot_x >= distance):
                rospy.loginfo("Robot Reached destination")
                rospy.logwarn("Stopping robot")

                break

        pub.publish(vel)
```

```
        rate.sleep()

if __name__ == '__main__':
    try:
        move_turtle(float(sys.argv[1]),float(sys.
        argv[2]),float(sys.argv[3]))
    except rospy.ROSInterruptException:
        pass
```

We can run this code by using the following command.

```
$ roslaunch turtlebot_gazebo turtlebot_world.launch
```

Start the TurtleBot simulation. If you are launching a file, you don't need to start roscore because roslaunch already runs roscore.

Run the move distance node with command-line arguments (see Figure 5-32).

```
$ rosrun hello_world move_turtlebot.py 0.2 0 3
```

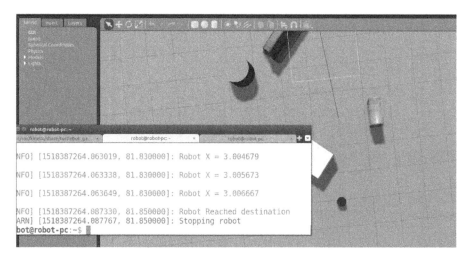

***Figure 5-32.***  *TurtleBot 2 moving 3 meters from its origin*

## Finding Obstacles

Using the same logic, we can find obstacles around TurtleBot. You can subscribe the laser scan topic from TurtleBot, which gives the obstacle range around the robot.

```
Topic: /scan
```

```
Message Type: sensor_msgs/LaserScan
```

Also, you get all the fields inside this message by using the following command.

```
$ rosmsg show sensor_msgs/LaserScan
```

A good exercise is to create an obstacle avoidance application in ROS.

# Programming Embedded Boards Using ROS

You have seen how to program a robot in ROS, and you have seen robot simulation. Now let's discuss how to create robot hardware and program using ROS.

One of the core ingredients of a robot is the microcontroller platform. A microcontroller is basically a chip on which we can write our own code. We can also configure the chip's pins. Microcontrollers are used for various applications. In robotics, controllers are used to interface sensors, such as ultrasonic distance sensors, IR sensors, and so forth, and for adjusting the speed of a robot's motors. Microcontrollers can also communicate with a PC via serial communication.

In this section, you look at some basic interfacing with popular microcontroller platforms, such as the Arduino (`www.arduino.cc`) and the Tiva-C Launchpad (`www.ti.com/tool/EK-TM4C123GXL`), and with single-board computers, such as Raspberry Pi 3 board (`www.raspberrypi.org`).

Let's start with the Arduino board.

# Interfacing Arduino with ROS

Arduino boards are on a microcontroller-based platform that program using a C++–like programming language. There are a variety of Arduino boards available (www.arduino.cc/en/Main/Products). We are going to use the Arduino Mega, which is available at https://store.arduino.cc/usa/arduino-mega-2560-rev3.

Figure 5-33 shows the Arduino Mega 2560 Rev3 board.

***Figure 5-33.***  *Arduino Mega 2560 board*

You can program the Arduino board by connecting to your PC. You can download the Arduino IDE from www.arduino.cc/en/Main/Software.

When you launch the IDE, you first see the window shown in Figure 5-34.

```
void setup() {
  // put your setup code here, to run once:

}

void loop() {
  // put your main code here, to run repeatedly:

}
```

*Figure 5-34.*  *Arduino IDE*

In the Arduino programming language, similar to C++, there are a lot of libraries available for simplifying tasks. For example, there are libraries for communicating with a PC, sending speed commands to motor drivers, and so forth.

There is also a library for interfacing with ROS. Using this library, the Arduino can send/receive messages to the PC. These messages are converted to topics on the PC side. Arduino can publish data and subscribe data, similar to a ROS node. Actually, Arduino acts like the ROS hardware node.

First, let's learn how to create an Arduino library for communicating with the ROS system.

We have to install a ROS package to create this library. The following is the command.

```
$ sudo apt-get install ros-kinetic-rosserial-arduino
```

This installs the necessary packages to interface Arduino with ROS.

The next step is to open the Arduino IDE. Select File Menu ➤ Preference. You get the window shown in Figure 5-35.

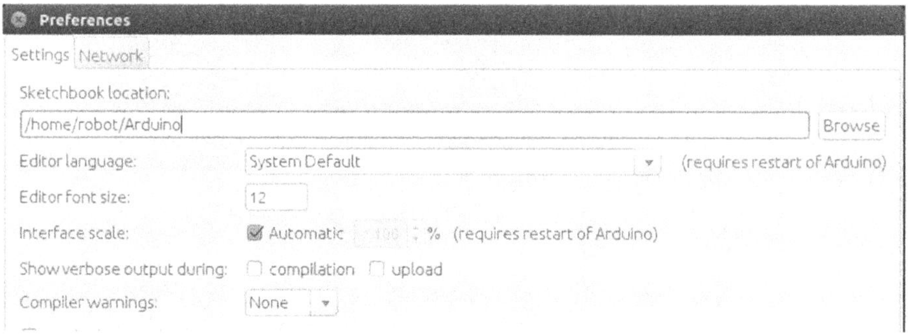

*Figure 5-35.* *Arduino Preference window*

Take a new terminal and switch to sketchbook folder path mentioned in the Preference Window. When you switch to this folder, you can find another folder called `libraries`. You can then switch to the `libraries` folder and execute the following command (see Figure 5-36).

```
$ rosrun rosserial_arduino make_libraries.py .
```

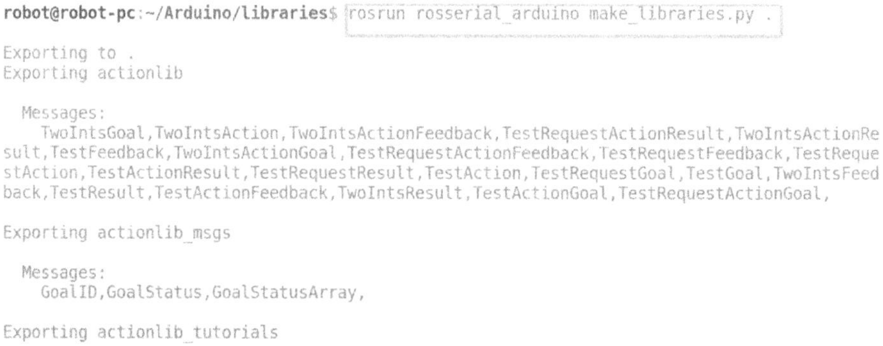

*Figure 5-36.* *Creating a ROS library for Arduino*

When you run the preceding command, you can see messages print on the terminal. This is actually creating the Arduino library for ROS.

After finishing the process, check the `libraries` folder. The `ros_lib` folder is the Arduino library for ROS.

Close the Arduino IDE and restart. Then go to File ➤ Examples ➤ ros_lib. You see a list of examples using Arduino and ROS. Let's discuss a basic example: Blink.

Blink is basically a Hello World example for the Arduino. When the Arduino interfaces with ROS, we get a topic. When we publish to a topic, it turns on, and when we publish again, its turns off. It is like LED toggling.

Figure 5-37 shows the Blink example.

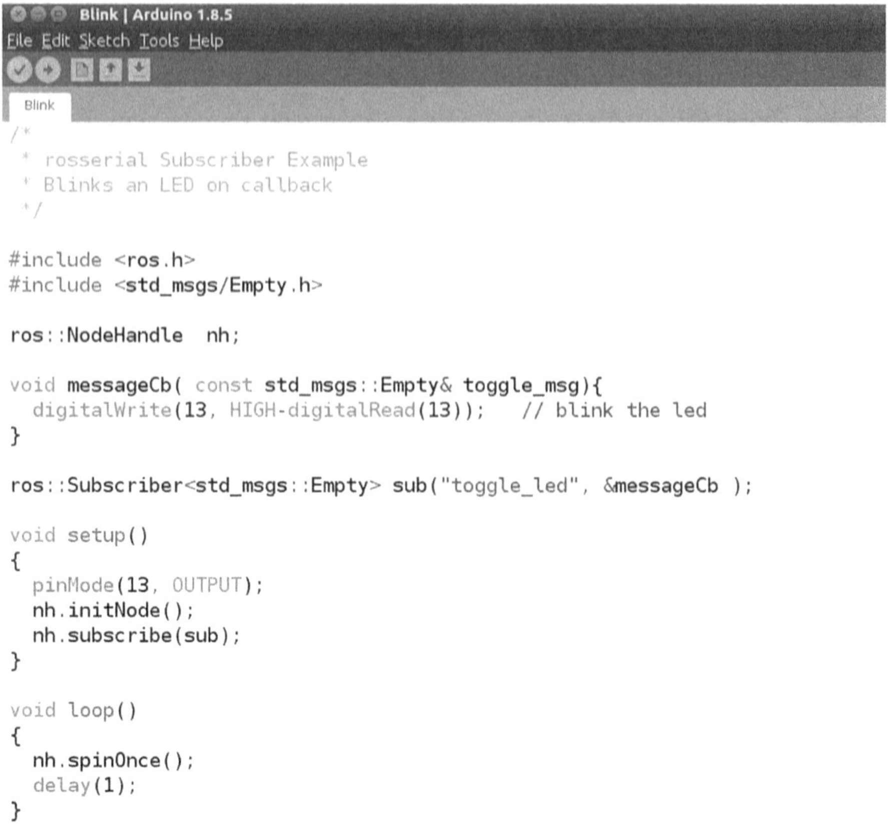
Blink | Arduino 1.8.5
File Edit Sketch Tools Help
Blink
/*
 * rosserial Subscriber Example
 * Blinks an LED on callback
 */
#include <ros.h>
#include <std_msgs/Empty.h>
ros::NodeHandle  nh;
void messageCb( const std_msgs::Empty& toggle_msg){
  digitalWrite(13, HIGH-digitalRead(13));   // blink the led
}
ros::Subscriber<std_msgs::Empty> sub("toggle_led", &messageCb );
void setup()
{
  pinMode(13, OUTPUT);
  nh.initNode();
  nh.subscribe(sub);
}
void loop()
{
  nh.spinOnce();
  delay(1);
}

***Figure 5-37.*** *The Arduino Blink example*

The workings of the code is self-explanatory. We create a node and subscribe a topic called /toggle_led. When a message comes to the topic, the LED turns on, and when next data comes to topic, the LED turns off.

Let's upload the code to Arduino. To do that, plug the Arduino to a laptop.

Find the Arduino serial port by using the dmesg commmand (see Figure 5-38).

```
$ dmesg
```

```
[  264.900785] usb 1-1.2: new full-speed USB device number 4 using ehci-pci
[  264.997219] usb 1-1.2: New USB device found, idVendor=2341, idProduct=0042
[  264.997230] usb 1-1.2: New USB device strings: Mfr=1, Product=2, SerialNumber
=220
[  264.997235] usb 1-1.2: Manufacturer: Arduino (www.arduino.cc)
[  264.997240] usb 1-1.2: SerialNumber: 753303039343516102F0
[  265.049964] cdc_acm 1-1.2:1.0: ttyACM0: USB ACM device
[  265.050611] usbcore: registered new interface driver cdc_acm
[  265.050619] cdc_acm: USB Abstract Control Model driver for USB modems and ISD
N adapters
```

**Figure 5-38.**   *The output of dmesg command*

The Arduino serial device is /dev/ttyACM0.

Change the device's permission by using the following command.

```
$ sudo chmod 777 /dev/ttyACM0
```

After that, select this serial device from the Arduino IDE.

```
Goto Tools->Port->ttyACM0
```

We can now compile this example and upload the code to the board.

After uploading the code, we have to execute the following commands to see the topics from the Arduino. Execute each command in separate terminals.

```
Starting roscore
```

```
$ roscore
```

Start the ROS serial server on the PC. The node does the conversion of topics to and from the Arduino.

```
$ rosrun rosserial_python serial_node.py /dev/ttyACM0
```

Publish a value to the /toggle_led topic.

```
$ rostopic pub toggle_led std_msgs/Empty --once
```

This turns on the LED on the board. If we do it again, it turns off. Figure 5-39 shows the output.

LED ON                                    LED OFF

***Figure 5-39.***  *The LED toggling command*

There are more examples of ROS/Arduino interfacing at `http://wiki.ros.org/rosserial_arduino/Tutorials`.

# Installing ROS on a Raspberry Pi

The Raspberry Pi computer is a popular board for DIY projects and robotics. The cost of the board is low, and its specifications are best for DIY projects. The latest Raspberry Pi 3 board has the following specs.

Name of SoC: Broadcom BCM2837.

CPU: 4× ARM Cortex-A53, 1.2GHz.

GPU: Broadcom VideoCore IV.

RAM: 1GB LPDDR2 (900 MHz)

Networking: 10/100 Ethernet, 2.4GHz 802.11n wireless.

Bluetooth: Bluetooth 4.1 Classic, Bluetooth Low Energy.

Storage: microSD.

GPIO: 40-pin header, populated.

The Raspberry Pi 3 is shown in Figure 5-40.

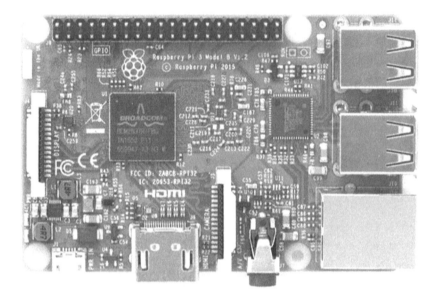

*Figure 5-40.* *The Raspberry Pi 3 board*

So how do you install an OS on this board and then install ROS onto it?

The next section explains the procedures for installing an operating system and ROS.

## Burning an Ubuntu Mate Image to a Micro SD Card

To install an OS on the Raspberry Pi 3, you need to buy a micro SD card that is greater than 16 GB. A micro SD card with class 10 is a great choice for the Pi.

There is a micro SD card that you can buy at http://a.co/1HyY8qr.

You also need to buy a micro SD card reader or an SD card adapter to plug into your laptop.

You can install the OS using the following GUI tool.

```
$ sudo apt-get install gnome-disk-utility
```

We are going to install Ubuntu Mate on the Raspberry Pi 3. You can download Ubuntu Mate OS from https://ubuntu-mate.org/download/.

Choose the Raspberry Pi option from the list. Download the image and open gnome-disk-utility. Select the SD card drive, and select the *Restore image* option. You can browse the downloaded image path here. A tutorial is available on YouTube at `https://youtu.be/V_6GNyL6Dac`.

After completing the restoring process, you can unmount the SD card and plug in to the Raspberry Pi 3.

## Booting to Ubuntu

After plugging in the SD card, plug a 5V, 2A supply to the Raspberry Pi 3, and connect Pi to an HDMI monitor. Also, connect a keyboard and a mouse via USB.

The system boots up, and you see the Ubuntu Mate desktop.

## Installing ROS on a Raspberry Pi

You can follow the ROS installation instructions at `http://wiki.ros.org/kinetic/Installation/Ubuntu`. These instructions are the same for the armhf platform, so it works well in Raspberry Pi 3.

# Summary

This chapter discussed programming with ROS. We started the chapter by discussing creating a ROS workspace. We saw how to create a workspace and how to create a ROS package. After creating a package, we saw how to write ROS nodes using C++ and Python. We wrote a sample ROS node using C++ and Python. We discussed ROS launch files and how to include our nodes in a launch file. We created a set of examples to work with turtlesim in ROS, and we worked with a Gazebo simulation of TurtleBot. At the end of the chapter, we saw how to program embedded boards such as the Arduino and the Raspberry Pi using ROS, which is very useful when creating robots.

The next chapter discusses how to create wheeled robot hardware and software using ROS.

# CHAPTER 6

# Robotics Project Using ROS

The previous chapter discussed programming using ROS client libraries such as rospy and ROSCPP. In this chapter, you see how to apply those things to a real robot. You see how to make a low-cost, differential drive robot that is compatible with ROS. You also see how to perform dead-reckoning in the robot using ROS. By doing this project, you get a clearer understanding of ROS concepts and where to apply them.

You are going to apply things that you learned in previous chapters, so you need to have a clear understanding of the last five chapters to do this project. You see how to assemble the robot hardware, how to interface sensors using Arduino, how to interface a ROS PC and a robot using a Bluetooth interface, how to create a robot model in ROS, and finally, how to write nodes to move the robot and perform dead reckoning.

## Getting Started with Wheeled Robots

Wheeled robots are a popular category of mobile robots. As the name suggest, wheels are used for locomotion. Differential drive is the most common and simple type of configuration used in wheeled robotics. In this configuration, there are two active wheels that move the robot and one or more passive wheels to support the active wheels. The active wheels have actuation, but passive wheels do not have any actuation. In this

© Lentin Joseph 2018
L. Joseph, *Robot Operating System (ROS) for Absolute Beginners*,
https://doi.org/10.1007/978-1-4842-3405-1_6

chapter, you see how to build differential drive robot hardware and write software to interface with ROS. From this chapter, you get a fundamental idea about interfacing a robot to ROS.

# Differential Drive Robot Kinematics

We are going to build a differential wheeled robot that looks like what's shown in Figure 6-1.

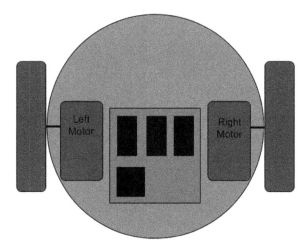

***Figure 6-1.*** *The differential drive configuration*

In differential drive, there are two wheels on the robot connected in the opposite direction. These wheels are attached to actuators that rotate the wheels once powered. Adjusting the speed of the motor moves the robot in different directions.

If the two motors are rotating in the same direction at the same speed, the robot moves either forward or backward. If the left wheel is static and the right wheel moves, the robot rotates around the left wheel and vice versa. If the two wheels are moving at the same speed but in opposite directions, the robot spins about its axis. Adjusting the speed of the wheel motors changes the position and orientation of the robot.

In this project, we are trying to move a differential robot from point A to point B. How do we do that? To achieve this, we have to calculate the exact position and orientation of the robot from the wheel speed. How do we calculate the speed of the robot's wheels? By using a sensor called *wheel encoders*. The wheel encoders count each revolution of the wheel. This count calculates the velocity and thereby the displacement and orientation of the robot.

The position and orientation of a robot can be represented as (x,y,z) and (roll, pitch, and yaw). The x,y,z represents the robot's 3D coordinates. *Roll* is the sidewise rotation of the robot, *pitch* is the forward and backward rotation of the robot, and *yaw* is commonly called the *heading* of the robot.

Consider a robot on a 2D plane. We only need to take care of three components to represent the robot position; that is (x,y,θ), where θ (theta) is the yaw, or heading, of the robot.

An illustration of x,y and theta is shown in Figure 6-2.

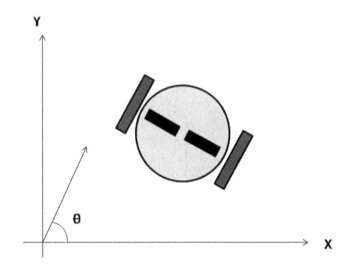

**Figure 6-2.** *The robot's position (x,y, θ ) in a global coordinate system*

To analyze the motion of the robot, such as predicting the current position and orientation while the robot is moving, we have to solve the robot's kinematics equation. Robot kinematics is the study of a robot's motion without considering the cause of it. There are two types of kinematics equations: forward and inverse. Kinematics equations vary by the type of robot.

In a differential drive robot, the forward kinematics is defined as follows: (x,y, θ) is the current position of the robot, and t is the current time. The kinematics equation can find the next position of the robot (x',y', θ') in t+δt, having known values of V-left and V-right, where δt is the small interval of time, and V-left and V-right are the velocity of the left and right wheels.

So how do we find (x',y',θ')? To find the future position of the robot, we can analyze differential drive robot model. Figure 6-3 shows the analysis of a differential drive robot model.

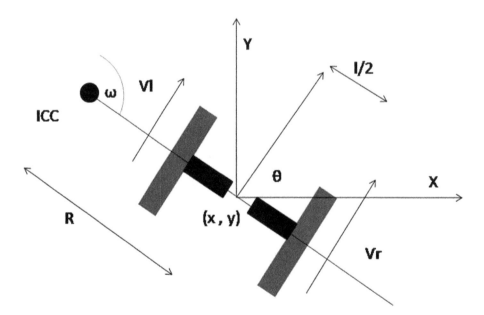

***Figure 6-3.*** *Analysis of differential drive configuration*

Figure 6-3 shows some of the robot's parameters. The two wheels are separated by distance, l. The velocities of the two wheels are Vr and Vl. There are three new terms: such as R, ICC (instantaneous center of rotation), and ω. ICC is an imaginary center point of rotation for both wheels. R is the distance from ICC to the center of the robot. ω is the angular velocity $(2\pi/180)$ (rad/s).

Figure 6-4 is another illustration of a moving robot configuration. ωδt is the angular displacement of the robot in a time step called δt.

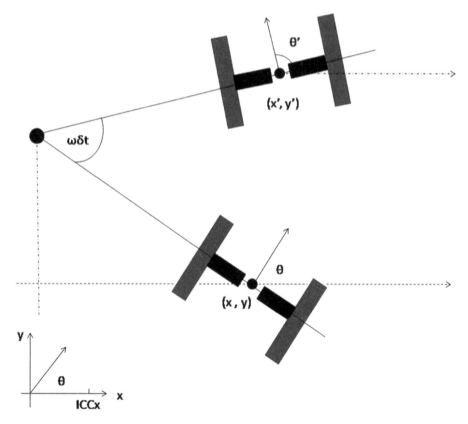

***Figure 6-4.*** *Analyzing the motion of a differential drive robot*

Figure 6-5 shows the equation to compute (x',y',θ'), and the equations for R, ωδt, and ICC.

$$
\begin{pmatrix} x' \\ y' \\ \theta' \end{pmatrix} = \begin{bmatrix} \cos(\omega\delta t) & -\sin(\omega\delta t) & 0 \\ \sin(\omega\delta t) & \cos(\omega\delta t) & 0 \\ 0 & 0 & 1 \end{bmatrix} \begin{bmatrix} x\text{-}ICC_x \\ y\text{-}ICC_y \\ \theta \end{bmatrix} + \begin{pmatrix} ICC_x \\ ICC_y \\ \omega\delta t \end{pmatrix}
$$

where

$R = l/2 \, (n_l + n_r) / (n_r - n_l)$
$\omega\delta t = (n_r - n_l) \, step \, / \, l$
$ICC = [\, x\text{-}R\,\sin\theta, \, y\text{+}R\,\cos\theta \,].$

***Figure 6-5.*** *Forward differential kinematics equations*

In the equation, $n_r$ and $n_l$ are encoder counts from each wheel. And step is the value corresponding to the distance the wheel covered for each tick of the encoder. So basically, we can compute the robot's next position from the robot's current position, encoder ticks, and fixed measurements, such as step distance and the distance between wheels.

You see how to implement these equations in ROS in upcoming sections.

# Building Robot Hardware

This section discusses the complete construction of a differential drive robot.

We are not making a robot from scratch; instead, we can buy a low-cost robotic platform and integrate all the sensors to make it work. We are using the standard two-wheel drive (2WD) platform, as shown in Figure 6-6.

*Figure 6-6.*  *2WD robotic kit*

# Buying Robot Components

The following lists the complete robot kit components that you need to purchase.

## Robot Chassis

The 2WD kit consists of a plastic chassis, a pair of plastic gear motors, a caster wheel (free wheel), an encoder disc, and the necessary nuts, bolts, and screws.

Figure 6-7 shows the components in the kit.

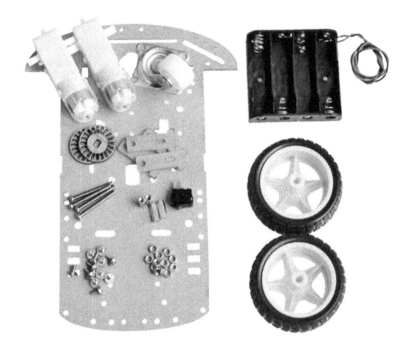

***Figure 6-7.*** *Components of 2WD robotic kit*

This is a common platform available at most online robotic websites, including www.robotshop.com/en/2wd-beginner-robot-chassis.html.

This robotic kit costs around $12 USD.

## Additional Motors and Wheels

We can either use the motors and wheels that come with the kit, or we can select motors and wheels with a specific configuration. Here we are using a 100 RPM motor with a 6.5 cm wheel diameter.

The motor and wheels can be purchased at http://a.co/7XyvdKh.

# Motor Driver

The motor driver is an electronic circuit board that adjusts the speed of the motor by feeding a pulse-width modulated (PWM) signal as input. We are using the motor driver shown in Figure 6-8 for this robot.

***Figure 6-8.*** *L-298 motor driver*

This motor driver board uses a 298N chip (www.sparkfun.com/datasheets/Robotics/L298_H_Bridge.pdf) with input voltage in the range of 5 volts to 35 volts, and a maximum drive current is up to 2 amperes. One motor driver controls the speed of two motors, so we only need a single motor driver for this robot.

This board can be purchased at http://a.co/0a3dJR8. This board is popular, so if the website does not work out, you can Google the board to find another website.

# Magnetic Quadrature Encoder

An important sensor is needed to measure the distance that each of the robot's wheels traverses. There are different kinds of wheel encoders available on the market. Optical encoders and quadrature encoders are commonly used. In optical encoders, there is an IR LED to detect the wheel rotation, but magnetic quadrature encoders use a Hall effect sensor to detect the rotation. The quadrature encoder can detect the forward and backward movement of wheels; for example, if the wheel is moving forward, the count increments; if it moving backward, the count decrements. In most optical encoders, however, we have to use our logic to detect wheel direction.

With this robot, we are using a simple magnetic encoder from DAGU. We also use the Hall effect sensor and a magnetic disk that can attach to the wheel shaft. Figure 6-9 shows what the sensor looks like and how to connect the magnetic disk to the motor shaft.

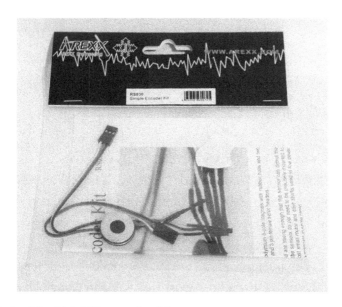

**Figure 6-9.**  *The DAGU encoder kit*

We are buying a low-cost encoder kit from DAGU. Figure 6-9 shows the encoder pack. It has two magnetic disks and two Hall effect sensors for a differential drive robot.

Figure 6-10 shows how to connect the wheel magnetic disk and the Hall effect sensor. Always check that the Hall effect sensor is near the magnetic disk.

***Figure 6-10.***  *Attaching the magnetic disk and sensor to the wheel shaft*

The cost of the encoder pair is about $10 USD.

You can buy the kit at `www.sparkfun.com/products/12629`.

The following website provides more information on types of encoders: `www.anaheimautomation.com/manuals/forms/encoder-guide.php#sthash.6YmwLmvD.dpbs`.

## Microcontroller Board

We are using the Arduino Mega 2560 board to control the robot motors and get sensor data. It is available at many online stores, including `www.robotshop.com/en/arduino-mega-2560-microcontroller-rev3.html`.

## Bluetooth Breakout

We are communicating with the robot using Bluetooth interface, particularly with a popular low-cost module called HC-05 Bluelink 5V TTL (see Figure 6-11). This module is directly compatible with Arduino. There are other breakouts available on the market, but it is working on 3.3V level, so you may need to use a level shifter to make it work.

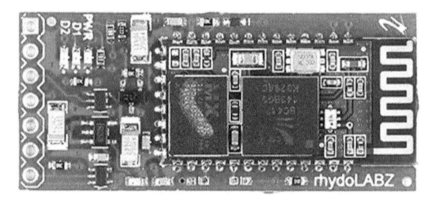

***Figure 6-11.*** *The Bluelink Bluetooth module*

You can order this module at www.rhydolabz.com/wireless-bluetooth-ble-c-130_132/hc05-bluelink-5v-ttl-p-1726.html.

## Ultrasonic Sensor

We are using a popular, low-cost ultrasonic sensor, HC-SR04, for obstacle detection (see Figure 6-12). If any obstacle appears on the robot's path, the robot will stop.

***Figure 6-12.*** *The HC-SR04 ultrasonic sensor*

The ultrasonic sensor has two units: a transmitter and a receiver. Computing the distance is based on the time required to receive the transmitted signals.

You can buy the ultrasonic sensor at `www.robotshop.com/en/hc-sr04-ultrasonic-range-finder.html`.

We only mount one ultrasonic sensor on the front of the robotic platform.

## Block Diagram of the Robot

Figure 6-13 shows the block diagram of the robot that we are going to design.

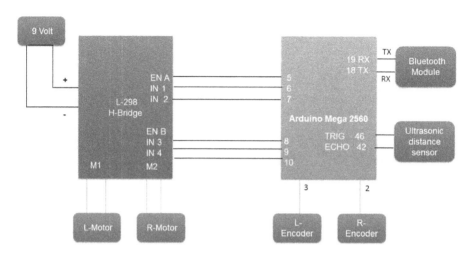

**Figure 6-13.** *Block diagram of mobile robot*

The two motors are connected to an L-298 H-bridge. You can connect one motor polarity opposite the other, because each motor is connected on opposite ends of the robot.

To control an H-bridge, several connections are needed between the H-bridge and the Arduino. The main connections are the enable pin and two input pins. The enable pin activates the current H-bridge and two IN pins determine the motor's rotation direction. There are a total of six pins controlling the two motors. The Arduino sends the proper signals to these pins to control motor movement.

The wheel encoders are the next set of sensors to interface. There are three pins in wheel encoders: VCC, GND, and output. VCC and GND can be connected to the Arduino VCC and GND, and the output of both encoders can be connected to the Arduino's 3 and 2 pins.

The Bluetooth module has four pins: VCC, GND, TX, and RX. TX and RX are the transmit and receive pins, respectively. You have to connect the Bluetooth TX pin to the Arduino RX pin, and the Bluetooth RX pin to the Arduino TX pin. VCC and GND are 5 volts, similar to encoders.

The ultrasonic sensor has four pins: VCC, GND, TRIG, and ECHO. The trigger pin is for transmitting the signal, and the echo is for receiving the reflected signals.

Let's discuss the voltage distribution for each component. The motors operate at between 5 volts and 9 volts, so the motor driver should power in in this range. All other components work in 5 volts . So you should be able to allocate your power in such a way that each component gets enough power; the GND of all components should be common too. We can power the robot through a battery or a 9 volt or a 12 volt DC adapter. The wired power supply is good for testing the robot.

## Assembling Robot Hardware

The completely assembled robot is shown in Figure 6-14. The Arduino, motor driver, Bluetooth, and ultrasonic sensor are completely wired and mounted on top of the robot. You can put the components together according to your logic.

***Figure 6-14.*** *Assembled wheeled robot*

# Creating a 3D ROS Model Using URDF

We are done assembling the robot, so now we can start programming it. The first step is to make the robot model in ROS, which is called URDF (Unified Robot Description Format). URDF has all the information on robot 3D models, robot joints, links, robot sensors, actuators, controllers, and so forth.

We are going to create a URDF model for our robot, which has the 3D representation of robot, a list of joints, and links.

The URDF is basically an XML file that has XML tags to represent a joint and a link (http://wiki.ros.org/urdf). Another representation of URDF is called Xacro (http://wiki.ros.org/xacro). In Xacro representation, we can create a macro definition using URDF. It can make our URDF code shorter and reusable.

A list of URDF tutorials is available at the ROS wiki at http://wiki.ros.org/urdf/Tutorials.

The following describes the basic usage of tags in URDF.

```
<!-- Definition of Robot link -->
<link name="my_link">
   <inertial>
    ........
   </inertial>

   <visual>
       ........
   </visual>

   <collision>
       ........
   </collision>
  </link>
```

```
<!-- Definition of joint  -->

<joint name="joint_name" type="joint_type">
    <parent link="parent_link_name"/>
    <child link="child_link_name" />
</joint>
```

Inside the `<link> </link>` tags is the definition of the robot link, which contains inertial parameters, collision parameters, and visual representation. The visual representation may have a primitive shape or a 3D mesh file.

The robot model created using URDF is usually kept on the ROS package; it is named `'robot_name_description'`.

The mobile robot's URDF package is kept in a package called `'mobile_robot_description'`. You can find this package in the Chapter 6 code folder. The URDF file is at `mobile_robot_description/urdf/robot_model.xacro`.

The following explains an important section in robot_model.xacro.

```
<?xml version="1.0" ?>

<robot name="mobile_robot" xmlns:xacro="http://ros.org/wiki/
xacro">

......................
</robot>
```

The URDF or Xacro are XML files, so the headers are the XML version, which is shown in the preceding code snippet.

Now, we can define the robot model inside the `<robot> </robot>` tags. The link and joint definition of the robot is inside this tag.

```
<link name="base_footprint"/>

<joint name="base_joint" type="fixed">
  <origin xyz="0 0 0.0102" rpy="0 0 -${M_PI/2}" />
```

```
    <parent link="base_footprint"/>
    <child link="base_link" />
  </joint>
```

In the preceding code, you can see the link definition of base_footprint, and the definition of a joint called base_joint. Normally, we create an imaginary link called base_footprint, which is acting as a reference for other links.

Following the 'base_footprint link', you can see the joint definition. A joint is a linkage of two links. The two links are 'base_footprint' and 'base_link'. The definition of 'base_link' is shown next.

```
<link name="base_link">
  <visual>
    <geometry>
      <!-- new mesh -->
      <mesh filename="package://mobile_robot_description/
      meshes/body/chasis.dae" scale="0.001 0.001 0.001"/>

    </geometry>

      <origin xyz="-0.07 -0.12 0" rpy="0 0 0"/>

  </visual>

  <collision>
    <geometry>
            <box size="0.14 0.23 0.1" />
    </geometry>
    <origin xyz="0.0 -0.02 0" rpy="0 0 0"/>
  </collision>

  <inertial>
    <!-- COM experimentally determined -->
    <origin xyz="-0.07 -0.12 0"/>
```

```
    <mass value="2.4"/> <!-- 2.4/2.6 kg for small/big
    battery pack -->

    <inertia ixx="0.019995" ixy="0.0" ixz="0.0"
             iyy="0.019995" iyz="0.0"
             izz="0.03675" />
  </inertial>
 </link>
```

In the 'base_link' definition, we can see the definition of the link's visual and collision parameters, as well as the inertial parameters. In the 'visual' definition, you can see that a mesh file is mentioned, which means that it shows as a link. The origin and orientation of the link are also mentioned. The mesh file is in our robot model. The mesh file in this section is a robot chassis without wheels.

The following code snippet shows how to define wheel joints. The wheel joint is a rotary joint, but in this project, it is a fixed joint. The following is only for visualization purposes.

```
<joint name="left_wheel_joint" type="fixed">
    <origin xyz="-0.06 0 0" rpy="0 0 0"/>
    <parent link="base_link"/>
    <child link="left_wheel_link"/>
    <axis xyz="1 0 0"/>

    <limit effort="100" velocity="100"/>
    <joint_properties damping="0.0" friction="0.0"/>

</joint>
```

The following code shows how to put a primitive shape in our model as a visual. There are several primitive shapes available in ROS. One of the models is a cylinder.

```
<visual>
    <origin xyz="0 0 0" rpy="0 ${M_PI/2} 0" />
    <geometry>
        <cylinder radius="0.0325" length = "0.02"/>
    </geometry>
    <material name ="black" />
</visual>
```

The robot model can visualize in Rviz. To visualize the model, copy the 'mobile_robot_description' package to your catkin_ws/src folder, and use catkin_make to build the packages.

Use the following command to view the robot model in Rviz.

```
$ roslaunch mobile_robot_description view_robot.launch
```

Figure 6-15 shows the URDF model of the robot in Rviz. You can change the camera view using a mouse in order to see the robot at different angles.

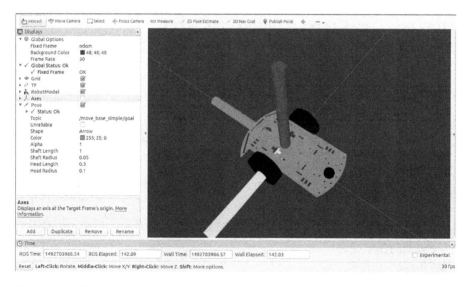

***Figure 6-15.*** *Robot model in Rviz*

We can also check the launch file to visualize the robot in Rviz. It is in `mobile_robot_description/launch/view_robot.launch`.

```
<launch>

<arg name="model" />

<!-- Parsing xacro and setting robot_description parameter -->
<param name="robot_description" command="$(find xacro)/xacro.py
$(find mobile_robot_description)/urdf/robot_model.xacro"/>

<!-- Starting robot state publish which  publish tf -->
<node name="robot_state_publisher" pkg="robot_state_publisher"
type="state_publisher"/>

<!-- Launch visualization in rviz -->
<node name="rviz" pkg="rviz" type="rviz" args="-d $(find
mobile_robot_description)/config/robot.rviz" required="true"/>

</launch>
```

The first step in the launch file is to load the Xacro file load as a ROS parameter named `'robot_description'`.

The robot_state_publisher node publishes the joint state of the robot model to /tf (`http://wiki.ros.org/tf`) topic. The `/tf` topic is useful for doing higher-level processing.

The next line of code starts the Rviz with a saved configuration file inside the `mobile_robot_description)/config` folder.

# Programming Robot Firmware

This section explains how to interface the robot sensors and actuators. The microcontroller board that we are using is the Arduino Mega 2560. We already wired the sensors to the appropriate Arduino pins. Now we have to write the code in the Arduino to take the value from the sensor to output some values and communicate to the PC.

The Arduino firmware is in the chapter_6/Arduino_Firmware/final_ code folder. It is actually lengthy code. We see some of the important aspects of the code and its algorithm.

We have to set up the prerequisites in order to compile the code.

We use two libraries to compile the firmware.

- New Ping: https://playground.arduino.cc/Code/ NewPing

- Messenger: https://playground.arduino.cc/Code/ Messenger

The library version used in this project is in the chapter_6/Arduino_ Firmware folder.

We have to copy these packages into <sketch_book_location>/ libraries. Now we can open the code in an Arduino IDE, and then compile and burn it to the Arduino board.

Let's have a look at the Arduino firmware code. Figure 6-16 shows the main logic in the firmware code.

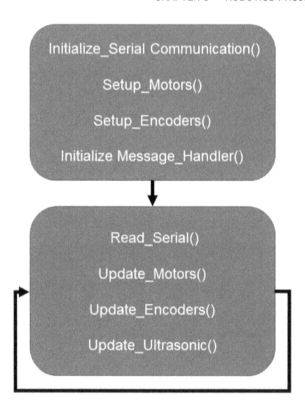

***Figure 6-16.*** *Arduino firmware code*

The first section of Arduino code to discuss is the Arduino `setup()` function. In `setup()`, we are actually initializing the sensors and actuators. The first thing that we are going to initialize is the serial communication. The current firmware sends all the sensor information to the serial port pins (TX,RX) of Arduino. The serial port pins interfaces to the Bluetooth module, so if any devices like PC or smartphone pairs to this Bluetooth module, that device can read all the data from the robot and can send commands to the Arduino. We are using a PC for communicating with the Arduino in the robot.

The serial communication between PC and Arduino initializes at a specific baud rate, and next initialization is for motor driver which interfaces the two motors. In this initialization, we are assigning pins in the Arduino in order send control commmands to the motor driver. We have to assign six Arduino pins for the motor control. Four pins change the direction of the two motors, and the other two pins control the speed of each motor. The speed controlling is done by sending a PWM signal to the enable pin of the motor driver. The PWM can be generated from Arduino pins.

The third initialization is for the encoders, which need two pins from the Arduino as an input that is configured as hardware interrupts. These two pins are Arduino interrupt pins, which generate an interrupt whenever a change in signal occurs in the encoder pins. The hardware interrupt pin number will be different in each Arduino boards. You have to check the Arduino board specification to find this dedicated pins. Using this method, we can count the pulse of the encoders.

The following code snippet shows how the encoder pins are configured.

```
//Motor EncoderLeft
pinMode(MOTOR_ENCODER_LEFT,INPUT);
digitalWrite(MOTOR_ENCODER_LEFT,HIGH);
attachInterrupt(MOTOR_ENCODER_LEFT_NO, Count_Left, CHANGE);

//Motor EncoderRight
pinMode(MOTOR_ENCODER_RIGHT,INPUT);
digitalWrite(MOTOR_ENCODER_RIGHT,HIGH);
attachInterrupt(MOTOR_ENCODER_RIGHT_NO, Count_Right, CHANGE);
```

The attachInterrupt() function in Arduino helps to create an interrupt on the corresponding pin. Note that the hardware interrupt does not support all the pins on the Arduino. We see that a limited numbers of pins are allocated for hardware interrupts.

The fourth part of the initialization is initializing Messenger_Handler, which helps with receiving the serial data and decodes that data in an easier way. We may need to receive a lot of commands from the PC. It is coming through Bluetooth-serial communication, so that message has to be decoded in order to extract the data in it. The Messenger_Handler is in the Arduino Messenger library.

Note that we are using the old version of the Messenger library for this project.

The following shows how Messenger_Handler initializes.

```
Messenger_Handler.attach(OnMssageCompleted);
```

The 'OnMssageCompleted' is a callback function executed when a serial message arrived on Arduino.

Given below the callback definition.

```
void OnMssageCompleted()
{

  char reset[] = "r";
  char set_speed[] = "s";

  if(Messenger_Handler.checkString(reset))
  {

     Serial.println("Reset Done");
     Reset();

  }
  if(Messenger_Handler.checkString(set_speed))
  {

     //This  set the speed
     Set_Speed();
     //return;

  }
}
```

We have to send a specific pattern of data as the Message library input. Then it can be decoded in the proper way.

The pattern is 'name value1 value2 valuen \r'.

So we can mention the name and the value of the name, and in the end, we have to append a carriage return ('\r').

In the preceding code, we used two names: "r" and "s". The "r" is for resetting the board, and the "s" is for setting the motor speed; for example, we can send the motor commands to the Arduino in the following way:

```
's 100 200\r'
```

The left motor speed is set at 100 and the right motor is set at 200.

After initialization, in the loop() function, we read the serial data using Read_From_Serial(), and give that data to Messenger Handler by using the following function.

```
Messenger_Handler.process(data);
```

After getting the serial message from PC over bluetooth, we can decode the speed and reset the command. In the same way, we are sending sensor values to the PC in another pattern. The pattern is 'name value1 value2 \n'.

The values of the wheel encoders, ultrasonic sensor are sending over Bluetooth to the PC.

This is main logic of the robot firmware.

# Programming Robot Using ROS

The main data from the PC to the robot is the left and right speed of the motor and the reset command. The data that we receive from the robot is encoder data and ultrasonic sensor data.

The sending and receiving of data from the robot is accomplished through a ROS node called the ROS Bluetooth driver node. It is actually a custom node written for this project.

The ROS Bluetooth driver node can communicate with the Bluetooth driver in Linux to receive and send data. After getting the data, it can publish topics. In the next section, you learn more about this node.

The nodes running on the PC are kept in a separate package called `'chapter_6/mobile_robot_pkg/scripts/'`. You can copy the `'mobile_robot_pkg'` to the `'catkin_ws/src'` folder and use `'catkin_make'` to build the package. The package does not have a C++ file, so the build process makes the package visible, and you can access each node from it.

## Creating a Bluetooth-ROS Driver for the Robot

You can find the Bluetooth driver node at `mobile_robot_pkg/scripts/robot_bt_driver.py`.

To run this node, you have to install the following Ubuntu package.

```
$ sudo apt-get install python-bluez
```

The python-bluez package installs a Python module called *bluetooth*, which has Bluetooth handling functionalities. We can use this module to access the Bluetooth device paired to the PC.

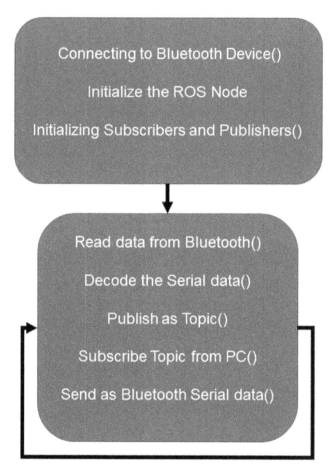

**Figure 6-17.** *Workings of the Bluetooth driver node*

During the initialization of this node, it tries to connect to the Bluetooth device. Use the MAC address of the Bluetooth device that you want to connect from PC. The Figure 6-17 shows how the ros bluetooth driver works.

To connect to the Bluetooth device in the robot, the robot should be powered on. You can pair the Bluetooth using a tool called *blueman* in Ubuntu.

```
$ sudo apt-get install blueman
```

You can install this tool by searching for "blueman" in the Unity search. After launching the application, you can pair the robot's Bluetooth device to the PC.

Figure 6-18 shows the Bluetooth manager in which you can search for the Bluetooth device and pair with the same.

***Figure 6-18.***  *The Bluetooth manager*

Once paired with the robot, note the MAC id of the robot's Bluetooth device and update that address in the bluetooth driver node, and then the node can directly connect to the device.

The following code shows the ros bluetooth driver node and explain how the Bluetooth module of the robot is access from the PC and establish the connection.

You can spot the following line of code to set the MAC id of the robot's Bluetooth address.

```
bluetooth_mac = '20:16:04:18:61:60'
```

The connect function in the code connects the PC Bluetooth to the robot Bluetooth.

```
def connect():
    global bluetooth_mac
    global bluetooth_serial_handle

  while(True):

        try:
            bluetooth_serial_handle = bluetooth.
            BluetoothSocket(bluetooth.RFCOMM)
            bluetooth_serial_handle.connect((bluetooth_mac, 1))
            break;

        except bluetooth.btcommon.BluetoothError as error:
            bluetooth_serial_handle.close()
            rospy.logwarn("Unable to connect, Retrying in
            10s...")
            #print "Could not connect: ", error, "; Retrying in
            10s..."
            time.sleep(10)
    return bluetooth_serial_handle;

bluetooth_serial_handle = connect()
```

The preceding code tries to connect with the device until you press Ctrl+C.

The following is a list of the publishers and subscribers defined for publishing the PC's sensor values and subscribing topics to send to the robot.

```
#Publisher and subscriber list

left_speed_handle = rospy.Publisher('left_speed', Int32, queue_
size=1)
right_speed_handle = rospy.Publisher('right_speed', Int32,
queue_size=1)
```

```
left_encoder_handle = rospy.Publisher('left_ticks', Int32,
queue_size=1)
right_encoder_handle = rospy.Publisher('right_ticks', Int32,
queue_size=1)

imu_yaw_handle = rospy.Publisher('yaw', Float32, queue_size=1)
imu_pitch_handle = rospy.Publisher('pitch', Float32, queue_size=1)
imu_roll_handle = rospy.Publisher('roll', Float32, queue_size=1)

imu_data_handle = rospy.Publisher('imu_data', Vector3, queue_
size=1)

ultrasonic_handle = rospy.Publisher('obstacle_distance', Int64,
queue_size=1)

#Subscribers

rospy.Subscriber('/set_speed', Int32MultiArray, speed_send)
rospy.Subscriber('/reset', Int32, reset_robot)
```

The following function is used to send data to the other Bluetooth device.

```
bluetooth_serial_handle.send(str(send_data))
```

The decode_string() function decodes serial data from the Bluetooth and stores it as a list. The publish_topics() function publishes the topics by reading the list already created by decode_string().

The decoding of serial data and publish topics is done in a continuous loop, and stops whenever you press Ctrl+C.

Figure 6-19 shows the topics published and subscribed by the 'ros_bluetooth_driver' node.

Subscribe Topics

Publish Topics

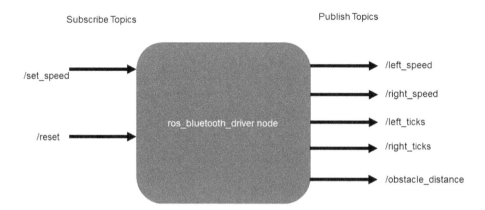

/set_speed

/reset

ros_bluetooth_driver node

/left_speed

/right_speed

/left_ticks

/right_ticks

/obstacle_distance

***Figure 6-19.*** *The ROS Bluetooth driver node publisher and subscriber list*

You can start the Bluetooth node by using the following instructions.

Starting roscore

```
$ roscore
```

Startin Bluetooth driver node
```
$ rosrun mobile_robot_ pkg Keyboard robot_bt_driver.py
```

# The Teleop Node

The purpose of the keyboard teleop node is to drive the robot using keyboard keys. This is used to verify that the robot is working and moving in the correct direction. It is similar to the teleop node used in turtlesim.

The keyboard teleop node is placed in chapter_6/ mobile_robot_ pkg/scripts/robot_teleop_key. This is Python code, and the teleop node is shown in Figure 6-20.

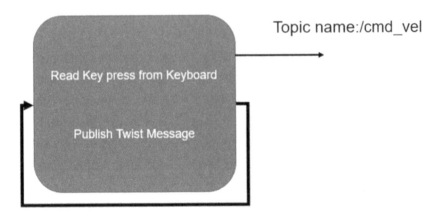

*Figure 6-20.* *The teleop node*

# The Twist Message to Motor Velocity Node

The twist-to-motor velocity node converts the ROS twist message (geometry_msgs/Twist) to motor velocities. The output of the node is a std_msgs/Int32MultiArray message with left and right motor speeds.

You can find the code at chapter_6/mobile_robot_pkg/scripts/twist_to_motors.py.

Figure 6-21 shows the input and output of the node. This node implements kinematics equations to convert twist-to-wheel velocities.

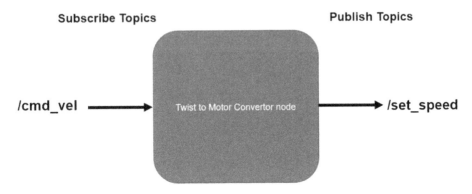

*Figure 6-21.* *The twist-to-motor velocity node*

# The Odometry Node

The odometry node is an important ROS node in a dead-reckoning project. This node subscribes the left and right and encoder ticks and computes the odometry data. The odometry data is the local position of the robot, meaning the position of the robot in respect to its starting position. We are going to use this odometry data to move the robot and rotate it in the desired angle. The odometry node implements the kinematics equation to compute the robot's position, which is the odometry data we are getting from the /odom topic (see Figure 6-22).

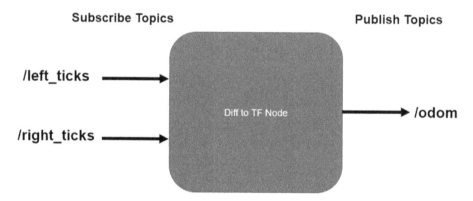

*Figure 6-22.* *The Diff to TF node*

The left and right ticks are the std_msgs/Int32 message, and /odom is the nav_msgs/Odometry message. You can find this node at mobile_ robot_pkg/scripts/diff_tf.py.

# The Dead-Reckoning Node

Dead reckoning is the final node discussed in this project. The node subscribe three topics: the odom to get the robot position, obstacle detection to avoid robot collision, and the /move_base_simple/goal, which is the destination of the robot.

Figure 6-23 shows the workings of the dead-reckoning node.

**Subscribe Topics**                                    **Publish Topics**

**/move_base_simple/goal**

**/odom**                          Dead Reckoning Node            **/cmd_vel**

**/obstacle_distance**

***Figure 6-23.*** *The dead-reckoning node*

After computing the distance to travel, this node sends the appropriate command velocity to the robot to reach the position. The goal pose is to get from the Rviz control panel. There is a dedicated button in Rviz to command the goal position.

The working of the node is as follows. When this node gets to the destination point as (x,y and theta), it sends a twist message to rotate the robot and align it to the destination point. The rotation is done by taking feedback from the 'odom' topic. After aligning with the destination robot, it sends a linear velocity command to move the robot in a straight line, while also taking feedback from the /odom topic to make sure that the destination is reached. If the destination is reached, the robot stops.

Currently, we are adding some tolerance to the destination point. The robot may not end up at the exact destination—there may be some drift, so tolerance in the goal position is added during the operation.

If there is an obstacle in front of the robot, the node takes the command velocity to zero so that the robot stops at that point.

# Final Run

In this section, you see how to test the robot. Make sure that the Bluetooth driver node is working well and getting the topic. If it is working, follow the procedures to start working with the robot.

Pair the PC Bluetooth and the robot, and start the Bluetooth driver to verify that the connection is OK. After that, quit the node and start the following launch file to start all the nodes.

Starting the robot stand alone launch file in PC

```
$ roslaunch mobile_robot_pkg robot_standalone.launch
```

This command starts running all the nodes and starts the Rviz using the following command.

```
$ rosrun rviz rviz
```

Open the configuration file at mobile_robot_description/config / robot.rviz. This shows the robot model, much like what's shown in Figure 6-24.

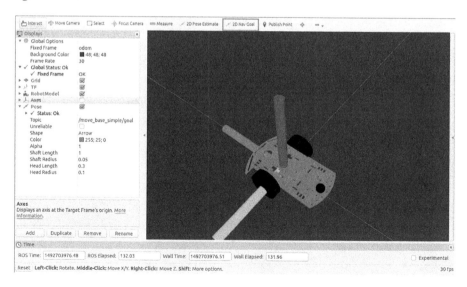

***Figure 6-24.***  *The dead-reckoning node*

Now you can command the goal position of the robot in Rviz using the 2D Nav Goal button at the top of the Rviz panel (see Figure 6-25).

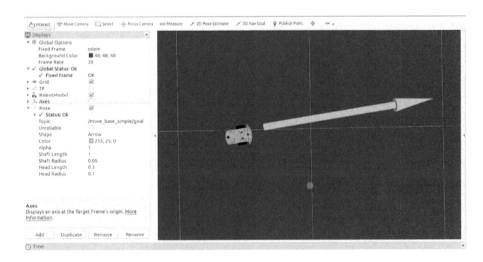

***Figure 6-25.*** *Setting goal position in Rviz*

The block diagram in Figure 6-26 shows the detailed interconnection of nodes in the dead reckoning project.

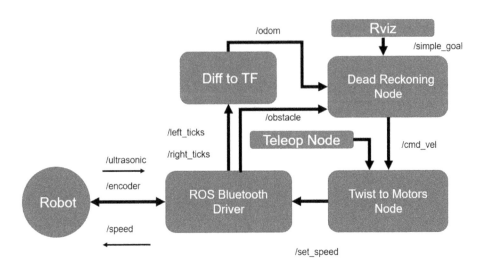

***Figure 6-26.*** *Interconnection of nodes*

If you want to simply run the robot, you can launch $ `roslaunch` `mobile_robot_pkg keyboard_teleop.launch`.

This launch file launches the Bluetooth driver, the twist to motor node, and the keyboard teleop node, which moves the robot using a keyboard.

# Summary

This chapter discussed a robotic project using ROS. The main aim of the chapter was to get hands-on experience with ROS on a real robot. The project was about creating a differential drive robot commanded from a ROS interface.

The chapter started by discussing the hardware needed to build the project. You saw the basic components to prototype the robot hardware. All the hardware components are available on the market at low cost. After properly connecting the robot's components, you saw how to create the ROS software for moving the robot. You saw how to create the robot's URDF model and how to write embedded code for controlling the robot. After that, you wrote ROS nodes in Python to receive the values from the embedded board and display in the Rviz tool. In the end, you saw how to move the robot using Rviz.

# Erratum to: Robot Operating System for Absolute Beginners: Robotics Programming Made Easy

## Lentin Joseph

**Erratum to:**

**L. Joseph, *Robot Operating System for Absolute Beginners*,**
**https://doi.org/10.1007/978-1-4842-3405-1**

The book title has been updated as Robot Operating System (ROS) for Absolute Beginners.

_____

The updated original online version for this book can be found at
https://doi.org/10.1007/978-1-4842-3405-1

© Lentin Joseph 2018
L. Joseph, *Robot Operating System (ROS) for Absolute Beginners*,
https://doi.org/10.1007/978-1-4842-3405-1_7

# Index

## A

Access modifier, 75–76
Arduino Mega 2560 board, 228–233

## B

Base class, 76

## C

Catkin workspace, 172
C++ language
  Bjarne Stroustrup, 56
  Boost libraries, 56
  CMake file, 92–93
  GCC/G++ compilers, 57
  installation, 57
  Linux makefile, 88, 90–91
  OOP concepts
    access modifier, 75–76
    classes and objects, 73–74
    classes and structs, 69–73
    data types, 69
    exception handling, 85–87
    files and streams, 82–83
    inheritance, 76–81
    namespaces, 84–85
    STL, 88

and Python, 55
verifying installation, 58–59
Client libraries
  Hello World
    building C++ nodes, 195
    CMakeLists.txt file, editing, 194–195
    C++ node, creation, 192–194
    computation graph, visualizing, 203
    launch files, 200, 202–203
    nodes execution, C++, 196–197
    nodes execution, Python, 200
    package creation, 189–191
    python nodes, creation, 198–199
  ROS CPP and ROS Py
    callback function, 187
    getParam() function, 188
    header files and ROS modules, 181–182
    initializing, ROS node, 183
    message definition, creation, 184
    NodeHandle instance, 184
    printing messages, 183

© Lentin Joseph 2018
L. Joseph, *Robot Operating System (ROS) for Absolute Beginners*,
https://doi.org/10.1007/978-1-4842-3405-1

# T

# U